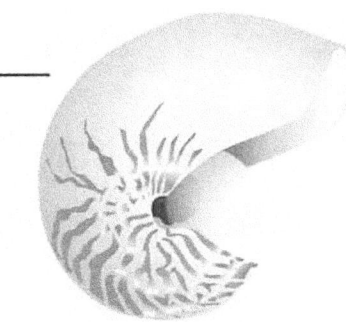

Coastal Marine Institute

University of Alaska

Population Genetic Structure of Common Eiders (*Somateria mollissima*) Nesting on Coastal Barrier Islands Adjacent to Oil Facilities in the Beaufort Sea, Alaska

Kevin G. McCracken
Principal Investigator

Co-principal Investigators:
Sarah A. Sonsthagen
Sandy L. Talbot
Richard B. Lanctot
Kim T. Scribner

Final Report
OCS Study MMS 2006-040
Prepared By Sarah A. Sonsthagen

August 2006

Minerals Management Service
Department of the Interior

and the

School of Fisheries & Ocean Sciences

University of Alaska Fairbanks

TABLE OF CONTENTS

LIST OF FIGURES

LIST OF TABLES

LIST OF APPENDICES

PART 1: Population Genetic Structure of Common Eiders (*Somateria mollissima*) Breeding in the Beaufort Sea, Alaska

Abstract

We assessed the level of population subdivision within the Pacific Common Eider (Somateria mollissima v-nigrum) breeding on 12 barrier islands in the Beaufort Sea, Alaska, using molecular markers with differing modes of inheritance and rates of evolution, as well as recapture data. Common Eider populations exhibited fine-scale population structuring based on all marker types. Regional comparisons between two island groups, Mikkelsen Bay and Simpson Lagoon, revealed structuring at 14 microsatellite loci (F_{ST} = 0.004, P = 0.016), mitochondrial DNA (mtDNA) control region (Φ_{ST} = 0.082, P = 0.047), and nuclear intron lamin A (Φ_{ST} = 0.022, P = 0.022). Given the geographic proximity of island groups (approximately 90 km apart), these values are noteworthy. Recapture data revealed substructuring between island groups, as we did not detect any female dispersal between groups (n = 34). In addition, inter-population variation in allelic frequencies was observed within mtDNA (Φ_{ST} = 0.135–0.271) and nuclear intron lamin A (Φ_{ST} = 0.089–0.173). Gene flow estimates based on microsatellite, mtDNA, and nuclear intron loci indicate asymmetrical western dispersal has occurred between island groups. Asymmetrical western gene flow may be driven by females from Mikkelsen Bay stopping early on spring migration at Simpson Lagoon to breed. Alternatively, young females arriving later may be forced to nest in Simpson Lagoon due to distribution of available nest sites. These data suggest that areas of genetic discordance can exist over very small spatial scales relative to the species dispersal capabilities and known dispersal distances.

Introduction

Microgeographic population structure is greatly influenced by natal and breeding dispersal. Here we define natal dispersal as the distance between an individual's natal site and the site of its first breeding attempt, and breeding dispersal as the distance an individual travels between each subsequent breeding attempt (Greenwood 1980). For many species, detecting natal and breeding dispersal is difficult, especially for mobile organisms that may travel long distances prior to and between breeding attempts. Advances in molecular techniques have made it possible to assess genetic structure of natural populations and evaluate the roles of contemporary and past dispersal events among areas (Newton 2003). Birds are of particular interest because most species that breed in arctic or temperate regions migrate to other areas during the nonbreeding season, and thus, show less geographic structure than other vertebrate groups (Avise 1996). Lack of population structure has been attributed to environmental variability of arctic and temperate regions, which increases dispersal and migratory behavior in birds, and can homogenize genetic diversity (Winker et al. 2000). Conversely, many birds exhibit high natal and breeding site fidelity (e.g., natal and breeding philopatry, respectively), which is expected to restrict gene flow among neighboring populations (Avise 1996), leading to population subdivision.

Differences in the degree of philopatry also may exist between males and females. The most common pattern in birds is for females to disperse farther between natal and breeding sites than males (Greenwood 1980). However, female waterfowl typically show greater natal and breeding philopatry than males (Rohwer and Anderson 1988). Males and females typically pair on the wintering grounds, and the male accompanies the female back to her natal area. Because ducks from different breeding areas frequently share a common wintering ground, males may disperse over long distances. Additionally, males may not mate with the same female each year, resulting in individual males breeding in distant locations from year-to-year (Anderson et al. 1992). Male behavior, thus, is expected to cause genetic mixing among individuals from multiple breeding areas, which may explain why many species of ducks are morphologically monotypic across the Holarctic (Newton 2003).

Patterns of natal, breeding, and winter site fidelity may leave varying signatures in molecular markers. Accordingly, researchers using genetic tools to investigate levels of spatial structuring and gene flow should use markers that differ in their mode of inheritance. For example, if females exhibit high natal and breeding philopatry and males disperse over large distances; there should be genetic structuring at the maternally inherited marker and little or no structure at bi-parentally inherited nuclear markers. If data were collected from just one of these genomes, gene flow among populations might be grossly over- or under-estimated depending on which marker type was used (Avise 2004). However, combining markers with different modes of inheritance and rates of evolution, researchers may ask a wider range of questions involving species population genetic structure and behavior.

Common Eiders (*Somateria mollissima*) have a circumpolar distribution and inhabit coastal regions throughout the Holarctic. There are 6 or 7 recognized subspecies that have partially overlapping breeding ranges (Goudie et al. 2000). The Pacific Common Eider (*S. m. v-nigrum*) breeds on the barrier islands of western Canada and Alaska (Johnson and Herter 1989, Johnson 2000), and has experienced a marked population decline (approximately 53%), since the mid-1970s (1996 population estimate 111,635 ± 42,440; Suydam et al. 2000). More recent surveys, however, indicate the population may have stabilized (R. Suydam, pers. comm.). Reasons for the decline are unknown. However, these birds are long lived with a low reproductive rate, which may be limiting population growth (Goudie et al. 2000). Long generation times could potentially increase extinction or extirpation risk (Marzluff and Dial 1991).

Rates of gene flow among breeding Pacific Common Eiders over scales relevant to conservation have not been measured. Satellite telemetry studies, however, indicate that adult female eiders that nest on islands in the Beaufort Sea may intermix with other eider populations during migration to wintering grounds in the Bering Sea south of the Chukotka Peninsula, Russia (Petersen and Flint 2002; L. Dickson, pers. comm.). Females that nest across large areas possibly pair with males from other breeding populations during winter, allowing gene flow through male-biased dispersal. Such gene flow would occur despite the observation that all transmittered females returned to their breeding areas in the western Beaufort Sea the following summer (Petersen and Flint 2002; L. Dickson, pers. comm.).

Data on degree of spatial population genetic structure are currently available only for the European Common Eider (*S. m. mollissima*) that breeds in the Baltic Sea. Tiedemann et al. (1999) found high levels of population structure among colonies in the Baltic Sea (133–1010 km) for maternally inherited mtDNA (Φ_{ST} = 0.262–0.343, $P < 0.001$), and significant, but lower, levels for bi-parentally inherited microsatellite loci (F_{ST} = 0.009–0.029, $P < 0.05$). The authors attributed high levels of spatial structure assayed using mtDNA to high rates of female natal philopatry. Proportionally lower spatial variance in allelic frequency at microsatellite loci was attributed to non-random mating by males on the wintering grounds (i.e., males mate with females from the same locality more often than expected).

Information on degree of spatial population structure for Pacific Common Eiders in the western Beaufort Sea is of particular interest to management and industry agencies because of the close proximity of nesting areas to oil and gas development activities (Minerals Management Service 2003). The phylopatric nature of Common Eiders (Reed 1975, Swennen 1990) coupled with nesting proximity to major industry infrastructure (Flint et al. 2003) makes this population susceptible to human disturbance (i.e. aircraft flights, personnel, etc.).

In addition, increases in numbers of avian and mammalian predators near oil development may adversely affect nest success and duckling survival (Johnson 2000). Effects of increased disturbances may be temporarily confounded as predators may avoid high use areas, potentially increasing nest success initially (Johnson 2000). Conversely, if increased disturbance causes females to flush from nests more readily, then nests would be more susceptible to predators. Subspecies risks can be exacerbated should genetically distinct populations occur in proximity to existing or proposed development. Thus, evaluation of population structure of Common Eiders in the western Beaufort Sea can provide means to assess potential risks of oil and gas exploration to the population or species.

We estimated levels of spatial population structure of Pacific Common Eiders breeding on the barrier islands in the western Beaufort Sea using microsatellite genotypes and sequence information from mtDNA control region and two nuclear introns, coupled with banding and genetic recapture data. Microsatellite and mtDNA loci have been used extensively to examine genetic discordance at fine spatial scales among waterfowl populations (e.g., Lanctot et al. 1999, Tiedemann et al. 1999, Scribner et al. 2001, Scribner et al. 2003, Pearce et al. 2004, Pearce et al. 2005). To our knowledge, however, this study is the first to use nuclear introns to assess levels of microgeographic population subdivision. Variation in nuclear introns, due to their higher effective population size, relative to mtDNA, and slower mutation rate, enables us to ask questions about historic processes influencing population subdivision (Hare 2001) occurring within the Beaufort Sea population. We hypothesized that the nuclear markers (microsatellites and intron sequences) would show little population genetic structure, because Common Eiders breeding on these islands share a common wintering ground with eiders from several other breeding areas. Over time, male dispersal among populations could homogenize allelic frequencies within the nuclear genome. However, we predicted that population structure would be observed at the maternally inherited mtDNA because of the high degree of female natal and breeding philopatry reported in other subspecies of Common Eider.

Methods

Sample Collection

Blood or feather samples from breeding female eiders and egg samples from nests were collected during mark-recapture and monitoring efforts on the barrier islands in the Beaufort Sea, Alaska, between June and July of 2000–2003. Samples were collected from two island groups, consisting of 12 islands in total (Fig. 1.1). The western group, hereafter called Simpson Lagoon, consists of five islands: Stump (70.419°N 148.601°W), Wannabe (70.437°N 148.725°W), Egg (70.440°N 148.739°W), Long (70.480°N 148.937°W), and Spy (70.564°N 149.895°W) islands (Fig. 1.1A). The eastern group, hereafter called Mikkelsen Bay; consists of seven islands: Camp (70.172°N 146.226°W), Point Thomson (70.186°N 146.325°W), Mary Saches (70.200°N 146.207°W), North Star (70.225°N 146.347°W), Duchess (70.233°N 146.405°W), Alaska (70.233°N 146.559°W), and Challenge (70.237°N 146.640°W) islands (Fig. 1.1B). Distances between islands within each of the two groups ranged from 1.2–49.2 km, and distances between islands located in Simpson and Mikkelsen Bay ranged from 78.1–143.1 km. Two islands, Camp and Wannabe, are not official names of islands on any recognized maps, but were given these names for the purpose of identifying areas in this study.

Females ($n = 198$) were captured on nests using a dip net during initial nest searching efforts or with a bow net during late-incubation (Sayler 1962). Blood was collected from the tarsal, brachial, or jugular veins and placed in blood lysis buffer (Longmire et al. 1988). Feather samples ($n = 114$) were collected from nest bowls from unsampled females and stored in silica gel desiccant at room temperature. Egg samples ($n = 15$ from 9 clutches) were collected opportunistically from abandoned or depredated nests or eggs that were cracked while trapping females. Egg membranes were placed in tissue preservation buffer (4.0 M Urea, 0.2 M NaCl, 10 mM EDTA, 0.5% N-Lauroyl-sarcosine, and 100 mM Tris-HCl [pH 8.0]; S. Talbot unpubl. data). Pectoral muscle and heart also were collected from eggs with developed embryos and stored in tissue preservation buffer.

After returning from the field, samples were stored at -80°C at the U. S. Geological Survey Molecular Ecology Laboratory. Genomic DNAs were extracted using either a "salting out" protocol described in Medrano et al. (1990) with modifications described in Sonsthagen et al. (2004), or a QIAGEN DNeasy Tissue Kit (QIAGEN, Valencia, CA). Genomic DNA extractions were quantified using fluorometry and diluted to 50 ng/μL working solutions.

Microsatellite Genotyping

Primers used for microsatellite genotyping of Common Eiders ($n = 327$; Appendix 1.A) were obtained via cross-species screening of microsatellite primers developed for other waterfowl. We screened 12 Common Eiders at 50 microsatellite loci reported to be variable for other waterfowl species and selected 14 microsatellite loci found to be polymorphic: *Aph*02, *Aph*08, *Aph*20, *Aph*23 (Maak et al. 2003); *Bca*μ1, *Bca*μ11, *Hhi*μ3 (Buchholz et al. 1998); *Cm*09 (Maak et al. 2000); *Sfi*μ10 (Libants et al. unpubl. data); *Smo*4, *Smo*7, *Smo*08, *Smo*10, and *Smo*12 (Paulus and Tiedemann 2003). Microsatellites were amplified using the polymerase chain reaction (PCR), and products were electrophoresed following protocols described in Sonsthagen et al. (2004) for tailed primers (*Aph*02, *Aph*08, *Aph*20, *Aph*23, *Cm*09, *Smo*4, *Smo*7, *Smo*08, *Smo*10, and *Smo*12) and Pearce et al. (2005) for direct-labeled primers (*Bca*μ1, *Bca*μ11, *Hhi*μ3, and *Sfi*μ10). For quality control purposes, 10% of the samples were randomly selected, re-amplified, and genotyped in duplicate.

MtDNA and Nuclear Intron Sequencing

We amplified a 545 bp portion of the control region domain I and II (Baker and Marshall 1997) using primer pairs L263 (5'-CCAAATYGCACRYCTGACAYTC-CAAGC-3') and H848 (5'-GCCCCATTATRTAG-GAGCTGCGG-3') approximately corresponding to positions 263 and 848 in the chicken mtDNA genome (Desjardins and Morais 1990). Only a subset of individuals, those for which we had blood samples, were sequenced ($n = 98$). PCR amplifications were carried out in a 50 μL volume reaction: 2–100 ng genomic DNA, 0.5 μM each primer, 1.0 μM dNTPs, 1X PCR buffer (Fisher Scientific, Pittsburgh, PA), 2.5 μM MgCl₂, and 0.2 units *Taq* Polymerase. PCR reactions began with 94°C for 7 minutes followed by 45 cycles each of 94°C for 20 s; 60°C for 20 s; 72°C for 1 min., concluded by a 7 min. extension at 72°C. PCR products were gel purified using a QIAGEN QIAquick Gel Extraction Kit and both strands were sequenced using Applied Biosystems BigDye v.3 Terminator Cycle Sequencing Kit diluted 4-fold on an ABI 3100 DNA sequencer (ABI: Applied Biosystems, Foster City, CA). Sequences from opposite strands were assembled using Sequencher 4.1.2 (Gene Codes Corporation, Ann Arbor, MI).

Due to the existence of nuclear pseudogenes in avian species (Sorenson and Fleischer 1996), we verified that the amplified sequences were mtDNA control region by comparing sequences from heart and blood samples from five putative mother and offspring groups. Since bird heart tissue is relatively rich in mtDNA and blood is relatively rich in nuclear DNA, any differences in sequences from mother/offspring groups are predicted to reflect the amplification of mtDNA and nuclear pseudogenes. Other studies also have compared heart, blood, and muscle to determine if primers are amplifying true mtDNA and not nuclear pseudogenes (Pearce et al. 2004). Common Eider sequences also were compared to those deposited in GenBank and individuals containing electropherogram double-peaks within mtDNA sequence data were re-sequenced. If co-amplified peaks were still detected at one of the 13 variable sites, presumably due to nuclear pseudogenes present in this species (Tiedemann and Kistowski 1998, S. Sonsthagen unpubl. data) or heteroplasmy, those individuals were removed (~10%). Sequences will be deposited in GenBank (http//:www ncbi nlm.nih.gov) upon publication of the results of this report.

Six nuclear introns also were screened for polymorphism in Common Eiders: beta-fibrinogin (*bf*) intron 7 (BF7F2 5'-GTTAGCATTATGAACTGCAAGTAATTG-3'; BF7R2 5'-TTTCTTGAATCTGTAGTTAACCT-GATG-3'; M. D. Sorenson unpubl. data), *lamin* A intron 3 (McCracken and Sorenson 2005), chromosome Z chromo-ATPase/helicase/DNA binding protein (*chd*1-W; Fridolfsson and Ellegren 1999), glyceraldehyde-3-phosphate dehydrogenase (*gapdh*) intron 11 (McCracken and Sorenson 2005), and ornithine carboxylase (*od*) intron 7 (OD7F 5'–TCGTTCAAGCCATTTCTGATGCC–3'; OD8R 5'-CCAGGRAAGCCACCAATRTC-3'; K. McCracken and M. Sorenson unpubl. data). Introns *bf*7, *od*7, and *chd*1-W showed very little variation within Common Eiders, with only 1–2 polymorphic sites in ten individuals. Two of the introns, *gapdh* (386–387 bp; McCracken and Sorenson 2005) and *lamin* A (280 bp; McCracken and Sorenson 2005) showed high levels of polymorphism (14 and 15 positions, respectively) and were sequenced using techniques described above with some modifications. PCR amplifications were carried out in a 50 µL volume; 2–100 ng genomic DNA, 0.5 µM each primer, and 25 µL AmpliTaq Gold PCR master mix (Applied Biosystems, Foster City, California). PCR reactions began with 94°C for 7 minutes followed by 45 cycles each of 94°C for 20 s; 64°C for 20 s; 72°C for 1 min., and ended with a 7 min. final extension at 72°C. Only sequences from the forward strand were collected on an ABI 3100 DNA sequencer because the PCR templates were short (280–387 bp) and sequences had a consistent electropherogram peak height throughout the length of the fragment. Sequences that contained double-peaks of approximately equal peak height, indicating the presence of two alleles, were coded with IUPAC degeneracy codes and treated as polymorphisms (Kulikova et al. 2004). Many sequences for *gapdh* contained a single recurring one base pair indel. To obtain data from the entire fragment for individuals that were heterozygous (~73%) for these alleles, we also sequenced the reverse strand. Sequences will be deposited in GenBank (http//:www ncbi nlm.nih.gov) upon publication of the results of this report.

Estimation of Genetic Diversity

To determine if the same individual was sampled across multiple years (between feather and blood or feather and feather samples), probabilities of identity for a randomly mating population (PID) and among siblings (PID$_{sib}$) were calculated in Gimlet 1.3.3 (Valière 2002) using genotypes from the 14 microsatellite loci. Samples with identical genotypes ($n = 9$) across the 14 loci and mother/offspring groups ($n = 9$) were removed from the analyses. For females that switched breeding islands among years ($n = 13$; 38%), we designated the island where the first capture occurred as a female's breeding population to maintain independence among samples.

We sequenced a subset of individuals for mtDNA and the two introns. Islands with low sample sizes were pooled based on geographic proximity (not greater than 3 km) of nests to neighboring islands. Samples from Challenge Island were pooled with Alaska Island, samples from Mary Saches Island were pooled with North Star Island, and samples from Wannabe Island were pooled with Egg Island. Allelic phases for *lamin* A and *gapdh* introns were inferred from diploid sequence data using PHASE 2.0 (Stephens et al. 2001). This program uses a Bayesian approach to reconstruct haplotypes from population genotypic data, and allows for recombination and the decay of linkage disequilibrium (LD) with distance. The PHASE analysis (parameters: 1,000 iterations with a 1,000 burn-in period) was repeated three times to ensure consistency across runs, as suggested by Stephens et al. (2001).

Using only adult breeding females, we calculated allelic frequencies, inbreeding coefficient (F$_{IS}$), and expected and observed heterozygosities for each microsatellite locus, mtDNA, and nuclear introns in GENE-POP 3.1 (Raymond and Rousset 1995) and FSTAT 2.9.3 (Goudet 1995, 2001). Hardy Weinberg Equilibrium (HWE) and linkage disequilibrium (LD) were tested in GENEPOP using the default parameters (Markov chain parameters: dememorization number 1,000, number of batches 100, and number of iterations per batch 10,000).

MtDNA control region and nuclear introns *lamin* A and *gapdh* sequences were tested for selective neutrality and historical fluctuations in population demography, using Fu's *Fs* (Fu 1997) and Tajima's *D* (Tajima 1989) in ARLEQUIN. Critical significance values of 5% required a *P*-value below 0.02 for Fu's *Fs* (Fu 1997). Unrooted phylogenetic trees for each gene were constructed in TCS 1.18 (Clement et al. 2000), which estimates genealogies using 95% statistical parsimony probabilities as defined by Templeton et al. (1992). *Lamin* A and *gapdh* intron sequences were also analyzed in NETWORK 4.1.0.8 (Fluxus Technology Ltd. 2004) using the Reduced Median network (Bandelt et al. 1995), to illustrate possible reticulations in the gene trees due to homoplasy or recombination.

Estimation of Population Subdivision

The degree of population subdivision among islands and between each island group were assessed by calculating global and pairwise F_{ST}, R_{ST}, and Φ_{ST} for microsatellite genotype and sequence data in FSTAT 2.9.3 and ARLEQUIN 2.0 (Schneider et al. 2000), adjusting for multiple comparisons using Bonferroni corrections ($\alpha = 0.05$) or permutations (3000) in FSTAT and ARLEQUIN, respectively. Fixation indices (F_{ST}, R_{ST}, and Φ_{ST}) mentioned above differ in the underlying model used to calculate values; such that, F_{ST} uses the island model, R_{ST} uses the stepwise mutation model developed for microsatellites, and Φ_{ST} uses a nucleotide substitution model that best fits the sequence data. Inter-haplotypic and inter-allelic sequence divergences were used to calculate pairwise Φ_{ST} (Excoffier et al. 1992). MODEL-TEST 3.06 (Posada and Crandall 1998) was used to determine the minimum parameter nucleotide substitution model that best fit the mtDNA and intron sequence data under the Akaike Information Criterion (Akaike 1974). Pairwise genetic distances between unique haplotypes and alleles were calculated in PAUP* 4.0 (Swofford 1998) for mtDNA and ARLEQUIN for nuclear introns. Additionally, a hierarchical analysis of molecular variance (AMOVA) was performed using ARLEQUIN to determine the magnitude of spatial variance in haplotypic and allelic frequencies among populations within and among island groups. An isolation by distance analysis was performed in IBD (Bohonak 2002), with microsatellite data and nuclear intron data using genotypic data inferred from the PHASE analysis, to determine if more geographically distant population pairs are also more genetically differentiated. IBD tests the statistical significance of the relationship between genetic and geographic distance using a Mantel test and calculates slope and intercept from RMA regressions following Sokal and Rohlf (1981) with confidence limits.

Finally, microsatellite data were analyzed in STRUCTURE 2.1 (Pritchard et al. 2000) to detect the occurrence of population structure without a priori knowledge of putative populations. Data were analyzed using an admixture model assuming correlated frequencies to probabilistically assign individuals to putative populations with 10,000 burn-in period, 100,000 Markov chain Monte Carlo iterations, number of possible populations (K) ranging from 1–10; this analysis was repeated five times to ensure consistency across runs.

Estimation of Gene Flow Among Populations

We used MIGRATE 2.0.3 (Beerli 1998, 2002, Beerli and Felsenstein 1999) to calculate the number of migrants per generation ($N_e m$) for microsatellite and nuclear intron data and number of female migrants per generation ($N_f m$) for mtDNA between the two island groups. Full models, θ ($4 N_e \mu$, composite measure of effective population size and mutation rate), and all pairwise migration parameters were estimated individually from the data and compared to restricted island models for which θ and pairwise migration parameters are symmetrical among populations.

MIGRATE was run using maximum likelihood search parameters: ten short chains (1,000 used trees out of 20,000 sampled), five long chains (10,000 used trees out 200,000 sampled), and five adaptively heated chains (start temperatures: 1, 1.5, 3, 6, and 12; swapping interval = 1). Full models were run three times to ensure the convergence of parameter estimates. Restricted models were run once. Competing models were evaluated for the goodness of fit given the data using a log-likelihood ratio test. The resulting statistic from the log likelihood ratio test is equal to a χ^2 distribution with the degrees of freedom equal to the difference in the number of parameters estimated in the two models (Beerli and Felsenstein 2001).

Results

Genetic Diversity

Bi-parentally inherited nuclear microsatellites

The number of alleles per locus at the 14 polymorphic microsatellite loci ranged from 3–44, with an average of 11.3 alleles per locus. The average number of alleles per population ranged from 4.93–8.21. The observed heterozygosity for each population ranged from 11.9–91.8% with an overall value of 57.7%. The inbreeding coefficient (F_{IS}) ranged from −0.071 to 0.060 across all islands with an overall value of 0.027. None of the inbreeding coefficients were significantly different from zero ($P > 0.05$).

Bi-parentally inherited nuclear introns

Twenty-five alleles for nuclear intron *lamin* A were reconstructed from 108 individuals in PHASE (Fig. 1.2A; Appendix 1.B). Sixty (56%) individuals were homozygous at all variable sites, and 22 (20%) individuals were heterozygous at one site. Using PHASE, probabilities of reconstructed haplotypes for individuals that were heterozygous for more than one site ranged from 0.82–0.99 ($n = 22$), except for two individuals with haplotype probabilities of 0.62, and 0.68. PHASE calculated the background recombination rate (ρ) as 0.50, with factors exceeding ρ ranging from 0.58–1.94 between 14 variable sites.

For nuclear intron *gapdh*, PHASE reconstructed 22 alleles from 88 individuals (Fig. 1.2B; Appendix 1.B). Six (7%) individuals were homozygous at all variable sites, and one (1%) individual was heterozygous at one site. Probabilities of all other reconstructed haplotypes ranged from 0.92–1.00 ($n = 57$) and 0.43–0.87 ($n = 24$), which may be attributable to potentially high levels of recombination occurring within this marker (0.39–4.41 factors exceeding $\rho = 0.05$, between 15 variable sites). There were seven variable sites that exceeded ρ by one or more factors: 2.12 factors between sites 16 and 22, 1.42 factors between sites 22 and 26, 1.12 factors between sites 48 and 49, 1.02 factors between sites 136 and 145, 1.11 factors between sites 165 and 170, 1.36 factors between sites 186 and 192, and 4.41 factors between sites 232 and 252.

Haplotype (h) and nucleotide (π) diversity ranged from 0.600–0.915 and 0.005–0.009, respectively, for *lamin* A, and from 0.874–0.954 and 0.006–0.009, respectively, for *gapdh* (Table 1.1). Observed and expected heterozygosity for *lamin* A was 41.6% and 87.9%, respectively, which significantly deviated from HWE ($P = 0.004$). Observed and expected heterozygosity for *gapdh* was 92.4% and 89.9%, respectively, which also significantly deviated from HWE ($P < 0.001$). Observed and expected heterozygosity for *lamin* A and *gapdh* combined was 67.8% and 88.6%, respectively, which significantly deviated from HWE ($P = 0.004$). Significantly negative values for Fu's Fs ($P < 0.02$) were observed for North Star and Mary Saches (*lamin* A -2.690; Table 1.1), Duchess (*lamin* A –4.704; *gapdh* -3.602; Table 1.1), and Long (*lamin* A –4.943; Table 1.1) islands, suggestive of population expansion.

Maternally inherited mtDNA

Eleven unique mtDNA control region haplotypes were resolved from 83 individuals (Fig. 1.2C; Appendix 1.B) defined by 13 variable sites. Haplotype and nucleotide diversity was high for most populations with values for haplotype (h) and nucleotide (π) diversity ranging from 0.000–0.891 and 0.000–0.009, respectively (Table 1.1). Spy Island was monotypic for mtDNA control region variation. Other islands were represented by 2–6 unique haplotypes, with Duchess Island having the highest number of unique haplotypes (Table 1.1). Neutrality tests found no evidence for selection (Fu's Fs = 0.090–2.139, $P > 0.02$; Tajima's $D = -1.295$–0.591, $P > 0.05$; Table 1.1).

Population Structure

Bi-parentally inherited nuclear microsatellites

After removing mother/offspring groups and identical genotypes ($n = 18$) at 14 microsatellite loci, the overall F_{ST} (global 0.004, $P = 0.007$) was significant. However, we did not observe a significant level of differentiation using a R_{ST} based approach (global -0.004, $P > 0.05$). Our overall estimate of population subdivision was low, and was not detected using the Bayesian clustering method implemented by the program STRUCTURE. The most likely model generated from the microsatellite data was maximized when the total number of populations was one. In addition, we did not detect any significant pairwise F_{ST} and R_{ST} comparisons among islands. However, the comparison between Mikkelsen Bay and Simpson Lagoon was significant ($F_{ST} = 0.004$, $P = 0.016$; Table 1.2). Moreover, a hierarchical analysis of molecular variance uncovered low but significant variance within populations and populations within a group using the F_{ST} based approach (Table 1.2). Finally, we found no evidence of isolation by distance correlations between genetic and geographic distances ($r = 0.012$, $P = 0.46$).

Bi-parentally inherited nuclear introns

Levels of spatial genetic structure for nuclear intron sequences were calculated using a nucleotide substitution model. MODELTEST indicated that the nucleotide substitution model that best fit the intron sequence data was the Tamura-Nei (1993) model with an invariant site parameter for both *lamin* A and *gapdh*. We detected significant differences in the spatial distribution of allelic frequencies for *lamin* A (global $\Phi_{ST} = 0.023$, $P = 0.02$) among islands. AMOVA detected significant variance among populations within groups and within populations (Table 1.2). A pairwise comparison between Mikkelsen Bay and Simpson Lagoon island groups also was significant for *lamin* A ($\Phi_{ST} = 0.022$, $P = 0.02$; Table 1.2). Inter-island comparisons indicated large significant pairwise differences within *lamin* A ($\Phi_{ST} = 0.089$-0.173; Table 1.3), but not for *gapdh* (global $\Phi_{ST} = -0.071$, $P = 0.94$; Tables 2, 3). As with the microsatellite data, we detected no significant correlations between genetic and geographic distances for *lamin* A and *gapdh* combined ($r = 0.096$, $P = 0.28$) or analyzed separately (*lamin* A $r = -0.012$, $P = 0.050$; *gapdh* $r = 0.142$, $P = 0.20$).

Since we observed significant pairwise comparisons within *lamin* A, we also calculated F_{ST} values for each polymorphic site in FSTAT. Significant F_{ST} values occurred at one of the 14 polymorphic positions: site 116 ($F_{ST} = 0.153 \pm 0.084$). Significant pairwise comparisons among islands were calculated for position 116, with significant F_{ST} values ranging from 0.053–0.352 (Table 1.4). However, site 116 is monomorphic for all islands in Mikkelsen Bay, therefore, the combination of several sites and the presence of rare alleles may be driving the observed population differentiation within Mikkelsen Bay.

Maternally inherited mtDNA

Population subdivision estimates also were calculated using a nucleotide substitution model. MODELTEST indicated that the nucleotide substitution model that best fit the data was the Tamura-Nei (1993) model with an invariant site parameter (substitute rate matrix: R[A–C] = 1.0000, R[A–G] = 34.6051, R[A–T] = 1.0000, R[C–G] = 1.0000, R[C–T] = 23.3368, R[G–T] = 1.0000, p–inv. = 0.8325, A = 0.2179, C = 0.3064, G = 0.1940, T = 0.2817). Mean inter-population variance in haplotypic frequency was low (global Φ_{ST} = 0.070, P = 0.05), along with a pairwise comparison between Mikkelsen Bay and Simpson Lagoon (Φ_{ST} = 0.082, P = 0.05; Table 1.2). Given the geographic proximity of these island groups, significant inter-population variances in haplotypic frequency (Φ_{ST}) of 0.05 are noteworthy (Wright 1951). In addition, we observed high levels of genetic discordance between Duchess (Mikkelsen Bay) and all four islands located in the Simpson Lagoon (Φ_{ST} = 0.135–0.271; Table 1.4). Finally, an AMOVA detected significant variance within populations and among populations within each group (Table 1.2), consistent with female philopatry over relatively short geographic distances (Scribner et al. 2001).

Estimates of Gene Flow

Analyses using the software STRUCTURE detected no population subdivision among samples, however, we tested a two-population model in MIGRATE based on geographic proximity of islands. Individuals breeding on islands located in Mikkelsen Bay and Simpson Lagoon were treated as separate populations (Fig. 1.1, Table 1.5). There appears to be asymmetrical dispersal between island groups in the Beaufort Sea across all marker types, though some comparisons (mtDNA and nuclear introns) are not significant based on overlapping 95% confidence intervals. The biases in the variances and the means indicate that, on average over generations, gene flow is greater from Mikkelsen Bay to Simpson Lagoon than vice versa (Table 1.5). $N_e m$ and θ values calculated in MIGRATE from microsatellite genotypes, mtDNA, and nuclear intron sequence data ranged from 5.1–24.2 migrants per generation from Simpson Lagoon to Mikkelsen Bay with θ ranging from 0.001–0.683, and 24.4–34.2 migrants per generation

from Mikkelsen Bay to Simpson Lagoon with θ ranging from 0.006–0.635 (Table 1.5).

The full model (all parameters allowed to vary independently) was found to have significantly higher likelihoods than the restricted island model (equal inter-population migration rate and equal θ across populations) for gene flow estimates based on microsatellite allelic, mtDNA haplotypic, and nuclear intron allelic frequencies (P < 0.001; Table 1.5), indicating gene flow is asymmetric between Mikkelsen Bay and Simpson Lagoon.

Female Site Fidelity

Analyses using the software Gimlet calculated an overall PID of 3.2×10^{-12} for a population composed of randomly mating individuals and 5.3×10^{-5} for siblings using genotypes collected from 14 microsatellite loci. These denominator values are much larger than the population breeding on islands in the western Beaufort Sea (approximately 500 nests found on the islands each year; Johnson 2000), which gave us confidence that identical genotypes for samples taken from different years were the same individual. Nine females were found to have identical genotypes; 56% had matching genotypes with feather samples taken on the same island in later years. Additionally, 25 females were captured in multiple years. The majority of these (n = 16/25; 64%) were recaptured on the same island. The remaining females switched breeding islands in subsequent years.

Throughout the course of the 4-year study, 34 females were detected breeding in two different years (based on observations of banded individuals and genetic techniques). Most (n = 21/34; 62%) nested on the same islands, whereas 13 (38%) females switched breeding islands. Inter-nest distances between breeding attempts ranged from 1.1–12.1 km using band recapture data (J. Reed unpubl. data), and 1.1–12.5 km using genetic recapture data. We found no evidence for female dispersal between Mikkelsen Bay and Simpson Lagoon. Females that did disperse to a different nest site between years generally moved to an adjacent island within the same island group to breed (9 of 13; 69%). However, three females breeding in Mikkelsen Bay moved from islands in the bay to islands closer to the coast (Alaska to Pt. Thomson Island, 12.1 and 12.5 km; Duchess to Camp Island, 10.2 km). One female breeding in Simpson Lagoon dispersed three islands east of her original nest site (Long to Stump Island, 10.0 km).

Discussion

Population Genetic Structure

Population subdivision was uncovered at all marker types. Comparably higher levels of structure were observed at maternally inherited mtDNA than bi-parentally inherited nuclear introns and microsatellite loci for inter-island comparisons, which is consistent with our prediction and known patterns of dispersal. The magnitude of differentiation decreased for mtDNA and nuclear intron *lamin* A when islands were combined into island groups, but it increased for microsatellites. Patterns of genetic structure were similar to those observed in Tiedemann et al. (1999); however, higher differentiation among colonies of similar geographic distance was observed. Tiedemann et al. (1999) proposed that the main mechanism promoting genetic subdivision among populations in the Baltic Sea was differences in migration phenology among geographic regions coupled with a selective advantage of early pair formation. However, differences in migratory phenology do not appear to occur among island groups in the Beaufort Sea, as satellite telemetry data indicate that there is no difference in the start of autumn migration among eiders breeding in the Beaufort Sea and Yukon-Kuskokwim Delta, Alaska (approximately 1250 km southwest of Beaufort Sea population; Petersen and Flint 2002). Lack of differences in migration phenology between island groups may explain, in part, the lower levels of differentiation observed as island groups likely admix on the wintering grounds.

Low levels of population structure resolved based on microsatellite markers were expected, mainly due to aspects of Common Eider breeding and wintering biology. Although female Common Eiders are reported to be highly philopatric to natal and breeding sites (*S. m. dresseri*, Reed 1975; *S. m. mollisima,* Swennen 1990), male eiders have large natal and breeding dispersal distances (0–1270 km; Swennen 1990). Tiedemann et al. (1999) reported evidence of non-random mating within Common Eiders breeding in the Baltic Sea, based on significant F_{ST} values, such that males tended to pair with females from the same breeding area among populations. We did not observe significant inter-population comparisons; however, our overall F_{ST} was significant. Additionally, we did detect significant genetic discordance in allelic frequencies between Simpson Lagoon and Mikkelsen Bay. Significant structuring, albeit low, at this marker could be a result of high female philopatry to island groups (Reed 1975, Swennen 1990). However, random mating on the wintering ground should homogenize gene frequencies in the nuclear genome through male-mediated gene flow (Scribner et al. 2001, Pearce et al. 2004).

Based on the number of nests found each year, Simpson Lagoon appears to support a larger number of breeding birds than Mikkelsen Bay (Johnson 2000, S.

Sonsthagen per. obs.). Scribner et al. (2001) indicated that unequal population sizes among studied sites could bias estimates of population subdivision. Individuals from populations that are larger would appear to mate assortatively, given the higher probability of mating with an individual from the same colony. Assortative mating among sites would have an upward bias on estimators of subdivision. Therefore, there could be greater gene flow than F_{ST} reflects. Though significant, our estimate of population structure is low enough to allow for high levels of gene flow among sampled sites. Satellite telemetry data from breeding female eiders, likewise, show that eiders from the Beaufort Sea share wintering areas with eiders breeding on the Kent Peninsula, Canada, western Alaska, and eastern Russia (Petersen and Flint 2002; L. Dickson, pers. comm., M. Petersen pers. comm.). Because individuals winter in admixed groups, consisting of many breeding populations, there is a potential for pairing of females from the Beaufort Sea with males from other areas.

The high level of population structure we observed within nuclear intron *lamin* A is surprising because we observed low to no population structure in the microsatellite markers and nuclear intron *gapdh*. As mentioned previously, our estimates of population structuring could be biased due to the assumption of equal breeding population sizes among islands (Scribner et al. 2001). Alternatively, we may not have observed high levels of population subdivision in the microsatellite data due to fragment size homoplasy. However, for the mutation process, and therefore homoplasy, to have an effect on estimators of population subdivision, subpopulations need to have different ratios of coalescent times of genes long enough to have two or more mutational events to occur (Estoup et al. 2002). Since our estimate of subdivision for F_{ST} (assumes migration is driving subdivision) was greater than R_{ST} (assumes mutation is the driving subdivision; O'Reilly et al. 2004) and because of the relatively close geographic proximity of the islands, mutation, and therefore homoplasy, is likely not playing a major role in differentiating populations of eiders breeding in the western Beaufort Sea. Moreover, PHASE estimated relatively low rates of recombination between variable sites within *lamin* A and higher recombination rates between variable sites within *gapdh*. The higher recombination rate observed within *gapdh* may have masked population structure among islands. *Lamin* A may be an "outlier" locus, as it may be in LD with a target of natural selection, which may have inflated Φ_{ST} (Storz et al. 2004). Charlesworth et al. (1997) stated that local adaptation tends to increase population differentiation at loci under selection, and very high F_{ST} values may be observed at closely linked neutral loci. *Lamin* A, thus, may be under balancing selection and coupled with genetic drift could create more alleles than what would be expected by chance. Low observed heterozygosity ($H_o = 0.416$, $H_e = 0.879$) and the larger number of alleles reconstructed by PHASE relative to *gapdh* (*lamin* A 70 alleles and *gapdh* 48 alleles; S. Sonsthagen unpubl. data) are consistent with this hypothesis. However, we did not find any evidence to indicate that *lamin* A is not selectively neutral (Table 1.1).

Comparatively higher levels of population subdivision assayed using mtDNA than nuclear DNA also could be attributed to lineage sorting. MtDNA has a lower effective population size relative to nuclear DNA. Therefore, when mutation rate and selection are held constant, genetic drift has a larger effect on mtDNA than nuclear DNA (Avise 2004), translating in higher estimates of population subdivision (F_{ST}). The effects of lineage sorting and sex-biased differences in philopatry on spatial genetic subdivision are not mutually exclusive and both may be playing a role in the degree of population structure observed. However, microsatellite loci have a high rate of mutation relative to mtDNA control region (Avise 2004) resulting in new mutations arising more frequently within populations. By chance alone, one would expect new mutations to increase in frequency among isolated populations and dampen the effects of incomplete lineage sorting within microsatellite loci. Given differences in the degree of philopatry in Common Eiders between the sexes and congruence in results between microsatellite and nuclear intron loci, differences in estimates of population subdivision may be more attributable to male dispersal and high natal and breeding philopatry in females rather than incomplete lineage sorting for the Beaufort Sea population.

We observed high levels of population structure within the maternally inherited mtDNA control region. Significant population subdivision was observed between Duchess Island, located in Mikkelsen Bay, and all islands located in Simpson Lagoon. While we did not detect significant pairwise comparisons among all islands in Mikkelsen Bay and Simpson Lagoon, we believe that the significant structuring observed is noteworthy given that Duchess Island is the only island that contains a colony of breeding Common Eiders in Mikkelsen Bay. Nests on the remaining islands were scattered with relatively few nests per island. The presence of a colony on Duchess Island is likely driving the significant pairwise comparisons observed at this marker. Common Eiders are typically colonial nesters (Goudie et al. 2000) and the low-density nesters could be "overflow" from Duchess Island, though demographic data are needed to confirm this hypothesis. Although there are also colonies on three islands in Simpson Lagoon (Egg, Long, and Stump islands), these colonies occur on islands that are adjacent to each other and thus unlikely to be genetically isolated, as birds may disperse among islands. While we do not have natal dispersal data for this population, we do have breeding dispersal distances from recaptured individuals. Given that no breeding females dispersed between Mikkelsen Bay and Simpson Lagoon, we hypothesize that females breeding in the western Beaufort Sea are strongly philopatric to island groups rather than to a particular island. This differs from observations of *S. m. dresseri* breeding in Maine (Wakely and Mendall 1976). Distances among islands in Maine are similar to those observed in our study (1.7–24.3 km apart), however, 71% of females returned to their previous breeding island, and only 2% dispersed to neighboring islands (estimated 27% mortality rate; Wakely and Mendall 1976). Over many generations, females dispersing among neighboring islands would have a homogenizing effect within island groups while maintaining population subdivision between island groups.

Behavioral responses to a more stochastic arctic environment may play a role in the differences in the degree of breeding philopatry observed between Maine and Beaufort Sea eiders. Common Eider nests in the western Beaufort Sea are associated with driftwood (Goudie et al. 2000, Johnson 2000), and changes in driftwood locations will affect where eiders nest. Storms dramatically modify the shape and topography of these barrier islands, thus changing where available habitat is located annually (Noel et al. 2005, S. Sonsthagen pers. obs.). Finally, eiders breeding on the Beaufort Sea postpone nesting attempts until the island is surrounded by open water, reducing predation risk (Schamel 1977). Islands located in the same vicinity may not be surrounded by water at the same time (S. Sonsthagen pers. obs.). Therefore, in years when ice break-up is late, eiders may initiate nesting on the first suitable island regardless of where they nested in previous years or hatched from because of the presumed selective advantage to nesting early (Milne 1974).

Gene Flow

We do not completely understand the factors that influence the degree of migratory and homing behavior in eiders. Eiders appear to move the minimum distance to wintering areas (Petersen and Flint 2002), and the degree of movement is likely environmentally induced (Swennen 1990), which may explain, in part, the directionality of gene flow observed at microsatellite and mtDNA markers.

Microsatellite and nuclear intron loci indicate significant asymmetrical gene flow, such that, on average, more individuals were dispersing from Mikkelsen Bay to Simpson Lagoon (i.e., east to west) over evolutionary time. Since eiders breeding in the Beaufort Sea share a wintering area with eiders from other populations, there may be clinal variation of allele frequencies occurring across populations that share wintering areas. Clinal variation at nuclear-based characteristics that may be under selection (e.g., plumage) has been observed in waterfowl and other avian species (Cooke et al. 1988, Smallwood et al. 1999). However, we did not observe a significant correlation between genetic and geographic distances. Therefore, samples from a larger geographic area are needed to confirm this hypothesis.

Asymmetrical gene flow from east to west observed for mtDNA appears to be consistent with estimates based on nuclear loci. Young female birds or failed breeders from the previous year from Mikkelsen Bay returning from the wintering grounds to breed, may stop earlier on their migration and attempt to breed at Simpson Lagoon. Islands become ice-free about two weeks earlier in Simpson Lagoon than in Mikkelsen Bay, likely due to the large volume of water flowing out of the Kuparuk River. This appears to expedite ice break-up on the nearby barrier islands (Schamel 1977, S. Sonsthagen pers. obs), enabling eiders to initiate nests and hatch broods sooner. Islands that first become free of ice produce the earliest broods in other populations (Ahlén and Andersson 1970). Should females from Mikkelsen Bay stop early on spring migration at Simpson Lagoon and successfully hatch young, they may be more likely to nest in Simpson Lagoon in succeeding years (Milne 1974). Thus, earlier nest initiation and previous nest success may be factors influencing females that hatched in Mikkelsen Bay to breed in Simpson Lagoon for the first time and then return there in successive years to breed. It is important to note that this pattern of westward dispersal would have to occur over many generations to be observed genetically. Thus, increasingly early ice break-up in Simpson Lagoon may have driven the westward bias in dispersal over evolutionary time. However, evidence from Common Eiders and other arctic nesting waterfowl suggests that young females initiate nesting later than older females (Johnson et al. 1992). Thus, open water may be present in both areas when young females are ready to nest, depending on the timing of ice break-up in a given year. Alternatively, Common Eiders may be dispersing west due to the distribution of available nest sites. Within the two study areas, Simpson Lagoon has more available nesting habitat relative to Mikkelsen Bay, based on the number of nests found in each island group in a given year (Johnson 2000, S. Sonsthagen pers. obs.). Female eiders hatched from Mikkelsen Bay arriving later to the breeding ground, such as first time breeders, may simply choose or be forced to nest in Simpson Lagoon due to

unavailability of nest sites in Mikkelsen Bay. This may be particularly true for young female eiders that tend to arrive later from the winter grounds as females arriving earlier on the breeding grounds may have already secured many suitable nest sites. Over evolutionary time, the limited availability of nest sites could also be influencing the dispersal pattern observed. It is important to note that one bout of random dispersal per generation among individuals breeding in the western Beaufort Sea could homogenize gene frequencies among islands. Therefore, western biased dispersal must have occurred over many generations.

Comparison to Other Waterfowl

The fine-scaled spatial genetic structuring that we observed in Common Eiders breeding on island groups 90 km apart in the western Beaufort Sea is exceptional, especially when compared to other arctic nesting waterfowl. Pearce et al. (2004) examined levels of population subdivision within the Holarctic nesting King Eider (*S. spectabilis*) using mtDNA cytochrome *b* sequence data and genotypes from six nuclear microsatellite loci. Estimates of inter-population allelic and haplotypic frequencies were not significantly different indicating panmixia across sampled sites in Russia, Alaska, and Canada. Stable isotope data from King Eiders suggest high levels of dispersal among western and eastern arctic populations (Mehl et al. 2004), which the authors contended is likely homogenizing gene frequencies among sampled sites. Levels of population structure also were assessed for Harlequin Ducks (*Histrionicus histrionicus*) breeding in Alaska (Lanctot et al. 1999). The authors did not detect any significant genetic discordance among sampled sites at four autosomal microsatellite loci, two Z-specific microsatellite loci, and mtDNA control region. Lack of structure was attributed to recent range expansion and thus insufficient time for genetic differences to evolve, stochastic events causing episodic dispersal, and low levels of dispersal among regions.

Among other waterfowl, population subdivision has been documented to varying degrees. Pearce et al. (2005) assessed population genetic structuring at seven microsatellite loci and cytochrome *b* mtDNA sequence among Steller's Eiders (*Polysticta stelleri*) breeding in Alaska and Russia. Low inter-population estimates of subdivision were observed at microsatellite loci ($F_{ST} = 0.002$–0.007). However, estimates based on mtDNA were not significant. In contrast, Scribner et al. (2001) documented high levels of differentiation in mtDNA among sampled sites in Spectacled Eiders (*S. fisheri*, $\Phi_{ST} = 0.242$). However, the authors did not detect any differences in allelic frequencies within the nuclear genome at five autosomal microsatellite loci and one Z-linked microsatellite locus. Canada Geese (*Branta canadensis*) also exhibit high levels of genetic differentiation among sampled sites at five autosomal microsatellite loci ($F_{ST} = 0.077$), one Z-linked microsatellite locus ($F_{ST} = 0.116$), and mtDNA control region ($\Phi_{ST} = 0.177$; Scribner et al. 2003). While these studies all documented significant differences in gene frequencies among sampled sites, studies were conducted at much larger spatial scales than our study.

Differences in the degree of population subdivision could be attributed to behavioral characteristics of individual species. Several aspects of the biology of many of these species are similar to that of Common Eiders, including: (1) exhibition of some degree of breeding site fidelity, (2) seasonal migratory behavior, (3) population admixture in large winter aggregations, (4) formation of pair-bonds in winter months with males following females back to winter sites, and (5) seasonal monogamy. In contrast to Common Eiders, many waterfowl species are monotypic across their range and show little to no population structuring (Newton 2003). Species that exhibit fine scale spatial structure, likely have high natal, breeding, and winter site philopatry, as has been indicated for Common Eiders (Goudie et al. 2000).

Conclusions

It appears that Common Eiders breeding in Simpson Lagoon are genetically differentiated relative to those breeding in Mikkelsen Bay, as we observed significant levels of population subdivision across all marker types. Therefore, Common Eiders breeding in each area may host populations that are demographically independent, though more demographic data are needed to confirm this hypothesis. Common Eiders appear to have high natal and breeding philopatry, as shown by the high inter-population variance estimates (Φ_{ST}) calculated for mtDNA and restricted female dispersal between island groups as shown by recapture data. In the event that a breeding area was extirpated it may be unlikely that the area would be easily re-colonized naturally by females hatched elsewhere, despite high levels of gene flow mediated by male dispersal (Wakely and Mendall 1976, Avise 2004). Additionally, these data illustrate an important point. Genetic discordance can exist on very small spatial scales relative to the species dispersal capabilities and known male dispersal distance. High natal philopatry observed in waterfowl, as seen in Common Eiders, can have demonstrable effects on the degree of genetic partitioning among populations.

This study was the first, to our knowledge, to use nuclear introns in assessing inter-population variation in

allelic frequencies at a microgeographic scale. Introns pose new challenges to phylogenetic and population genetic analysis, such as recombination impeding gene tree reconstruction (Hare 2001) and selective sweeps potentially confounding gene flow estimates (Storz et al. 2004). However, high levels of variation found in loci potentially under balancing selection can provide valuable insight on historic processes influencing population demography. Advancements in analytical tools have enabled researchers to address issues of recombination (e.g., PHASE) and selective sweeps (DetSel, Vitalis et al. 2003; Fu's *Fs*, Tajima's *D* in ARLEQUIN) and use these types of markers for population genetic analyses. Finally, these data provide further evidence for the need to use multiple marker types with varying modes of inheritance. If researchers were to restrict their investigation to either nuclear or mtDNA markers when genetically characterizing populations, studies could under or over estimate levels of population structure. As seen in Common Eiders, nuclear and mtDNA markers show varying levels of genetic spatial partitioning. Not utilizing molecular markers with different modes of inheritance and evolution could mislead researchers characterizing the genetic variation within this population.

Acknowledgments

Funding was provided by: Minerals Management Service (1435-01-98-CA-30909); Coastal Marine Institute, University of Alaska Fairbanks; U. S. Geological Survey; Alaska EPSCoR Graduate Fellowship (NSF EPS-0092040); University of Alaska Foundation Angus Gavin Migratory Bird Research Fund; and BP Exploration (Alaska) Inc. We thank all of the U. S. Geological Survey researchers and biologists that worked on the Beaufort Sea Common Eider project, especially P. Flint, J. C. Franson, D. LaCroix, and J. Reed, as well as, J. Gust and G. K. Sage, who provided laboratory assistance. J. Gleason, C. Monnett, J. Pearce, M. Petersen, and J. Gust, U. S. Geological Survey, and four anonymous reviewers, provided valuable comments on earlier drafts of this manuscript.

The USFWS banding number for the USGS is 20022 and the master permit holder is Dirk Derksen. The IACUC number #02-01 was assigned for this work to Kevin McCrackin.

References

Ahlén, I., and Å. Andersson. 1970. Breeding ecology of an eider population on Spitsbergen. Ornis Scand. 1:83–106.

Akaike, H. 1974. A new look at the statistical model

identification. IEEE Trans. Automat. Contr. 19(6):716–723.

Anderson, M.G., J.M. Rhymer and F.C. Rohwer. 1992. Philopatry, dispersal, and the genetic structure of waterfowl populations, p. 365–395. *In* B.D.J. Batt, A.D. Afton, M.G. Anderson, C.D. Ankney, D.H. Johnson, J.A. Kadlec and G.L. Krapu [eds.], Ecology and Management of Breeding Waterfowl. University of Minnesota Press, Minneapolis, Minnesota.

Avise, J.C. 1996. Three fundamental contributions of molecular genetics to avian ecology and evolution. Ibis 138(1):16–25.

Avise, J.C. 2004. Molecular Markers, Natural History, and Evolution. Second Edition. Sinauer Associates, Inc., Sunderland, Massachusetts.

Baker, A.J., and H.D. Marshall. 1997. Mitochondrial control region sequences as tools for understanding evolution, p. 51–82. *In* D.P. Mindell [ed.], Avian Molecular Evolution and Systematics. Academic Press, San Diego, California.

Bandelt, H.J., P. Forster, B.C. Sykes and M.B. Richards. 1995. Mitochondrial portraits of human populations using median networks. Genetics 141(2):743–753.

Beerli, P. 1998. Estimation of migration rates and population sizes in geographically structured populations, p. 39–53. *In* G.R. Carvalho [ed.], Advances in Molecular Ecology. NATO Science Series: Life Sciences, Vol. 306. IOS Press, Amsterdam, The Netherlands.

Beerli, P. 2002. LAMARC – Likelihood Analysis with Metropolis Algorithm using Random Coalescence. Available at http://evolution.genetics.washington.edu/lamarc/index html (accessed 7 July 2004).

Beerli, P., and J. Felsenstein. 1999. Maximum-likelihood estimation of migration rates and effective population numbers in two populations using a coalescent approach. Genetics 152(2):763–773.

Beerli, P., and J. Felsenstein. 2001. Maximum likelihood estimation of a migration matrix and effective population sizes in *n* subpopulations by using a coalescent approach. Proc. Natl. Acad. Sci. USA 98(8):4563–4568. doi: 10.1073/pnas.081068098

Bohonak, A.J. 2002. IBD (Isolation by Distance): A program for analyses of isolation by distance. J. Heredity 93(2):153–154. doi: 10.1093/jhered/93.2.153

Buchholz, W.G., J.M. Pearce, B.J. Pierson and K.T. Scribner. 1998. Dinucleotide repeat polymorphisms in waterfowl (family Anatidae): Characterization of a sex-linked (*Z*-specific) and 14 autosomal loci. Anim. Genet. 29(4):323–325.

Charlesworth, B., M. Nordborg and D. Charlesworth. 1997. The effects of local selection, balanced polymorphism and background selection on equilibrium patterns of genetic diversity in subdivided populations. Genetical Res. 70(2):155–174.

Clement, M., D. Posada and K.A. Crandall. 2000. TCS: A computer program to estimate gene genealogies. Mol. Ecol. 9(10):1657–1660. doi: 10.1046/j.1365-294x.2000.01020.x

Cooke, F., D.T. Parkin and R.F. Rockwell. 1988. Evidence of former allopatry of the two color phases of Lesser Snow Geese (*Chen caerulescens caerulescens*). Auk 105(3):467–479.

Desjardins, P., and R. Morais. 1990. Sequence and gene organization of the chicken mitochondrial genome. A novel gene order in higher vertebrates. J. Mol. Biol. 212(4):599–634.

Estoup, A., P. Jarne and J.-M. Cornuet. 2002. Homoplasy and mutation model at microsatellite loci and their consequences for population genetics analysis. Mol. Ecol. 11(9):1591–1604. doi: 10.1046/j.1365-294X.2002.01576.x

Excoffier, L., P.E. Smouse and J.M. Quatro. 1992. Analysis of molecular variance inferred from metric distances among DNA haplotypes: Application to human mitochondrial DNA restriction data. Genetics 131(2):479–491.

Flint, P.L., J.A. Reed, J.C. Franson, T.E. Hollmén, J.B. Grand, M.D. Howell, R.B. Lanctot, D.L. Lacroix and C.P. Dau. 2003. Monitoring Beaufort Sea Waterfowl and Marine Birds. OCS Study MMS 2003-037, U.S. Geological Survey, Alaska Science Center, Anchorage and USDOI, MMS, Alaska OCS Region, 125 p.

Fluxus Technology Ltd. 2004. Network 4.1.0.8. Available online at http://www.fluxus-engineering.com

Fridolfsson A.-K., and H. Ellegren. 1999. A simple and universal method for molecular sexing of non-ratite birds. J. Avian Biol. 30(1):116–121.

Fu, Y.X. 1997. Statistical tests of neutrality of mutations against population growth, hitchhiking and background selections. Genetics 147(2):915–925.

Goudet, J. 1995. FSTAT (version 1.2): A computer program to calculate F-statistics. J. Heredity 86(6):485–486.

Goudet, J. 2001. FSTAT, a program to estimate and test gene diversities and fixation indices (version 2.9.3.2). Available at http://www2.unil.ch/popgen/softwares/fstat htm (accessed 7 July 2004).

Goudie, R.I., G.J. Robertson and A. Reed. 2000. Common Eider (*Somateria mollissima*), The Birds of North America, No. 546 [A. Poole and F. Gill, eds.]. The Birds of North America, Inc., Philadelphia, Pennsylvania, 32 p.

Greenwood, P.J. 1980. Mating systems, philopatry and dispersal in birds and mammals. Anim. Behav. 28:1140–1162.

Hare, M.P. 2001. Prospects for nuclear gene phylogeography. Trends Ecol. Evol. 16(12):700–706.

Johnson, D.H., J.D. Nichols and M.D. Schwartz. 1992. Population dynamics of breeding waterfowl, p. 446–485. *In* B.D.J. Batt, A.D. Afton, M.G. Anderson, C.D. Ankney, D.H. Johnson, J.A. Kadlec and G.L. Krapu [eds.], Ecology and Management of Breeding Waterfowl. University of Minnesota Press, Minneapolis, Minnesota.

Johnson, S.R. 2000. Pacific Eider, p. 259–275. *In* J.C. Truett and S.R. Johnson [eds.], The Natural History of an Arctic Oil Field: Development and the Biota. Academic Press, San Diego, California.

Johnson, S.R., and D.R. Herter. 1989. The Birds of the Beaufort Sea. BP Exploration (Alaska) Inc., Anchorage, Alaska, 372 p.

Kulikova, I.V., Y.N. Zhuravlev and K.G. McCracken. 2004. Asymmetric hybridization and sex-biased gene flow between Eastern Spot-billed Ducks (*Anas zonorhyncha*) and Mallards (*A. platyrhynchos*) in the Russian Far East. Auk 121(3):930–949. doi: 10.1642/0004-8038(2004)121[0930:AHASGF]2.0.CO;2

Lanctot, R., B. Goatcher, K. Scribner, S. Talbot, B. Pierson, D. Esler and D. Zwiefelhofer. 1999. Harlequin Duck recovery from the *Exxon Valdez* oil spill: A population genetics perspective. Auk 116(3):781–791.

Longmire, J.L., A.K. Lewis, N.C. Brown, J.M. Buckingham, L.M. Clark, M.D. Jones, L.J. Meincke, J. Meyne, R.L. Ratliff, F.A. Ray, R.P. Wagner and R.K. Moyzis. 1988. Isolation and molecular characterization of a highly polymorphic centromeric tandem repeat in the family Falconidae. Genomics 2(1):14–24.

Maak, S., K. Neumann, G. von Lengerken and R. Gattermann. 2000. First seven microsatellites developed for the Peking duck (*Anas platyrhynchos*). Anim. Genet. 31(3):233.

Maak, S., K. Wimmers, S. Weigend and K. Neumann. 2003. Isolation and characterization of 18 microsatellites in the Peking duck (*Anas platyrhynchos*) and their application in other waterfowl species.

Mol. Ecol. Notes 3(2):224–227. doi: 10.1046/j.1471-8286.2003.00405.x

Marzluff, J.M., and K.P. Dial. 1991. Life history correlates of taxonomic diversity. Ecology 72(2):428–439.

McCracken, K.G., and M.D. Sorenson. 2005. Is homoplasy or lineage sorting the source of incongruent mtDNA and nuclear gene trees in the stiff-tailed ducks (*Nomonyx-Oxyura*)? Syst. Biol. 54(1):35–55. doi: 10.1080/10635150590910249

Medrano J.F., E. Aasen, and L. Sharrow. 1990. DNA extraction from nucleated red blood cells. Biotechniques 8(1):43. Mehl, K.R., R.T. Alisauskas, K.A. Hobson and D.K. Kellett. 2004. To winter east or west? Heterogeneity in winter philopatry in a central-arctic population of King Eiders. Condor 106(2):241–251. doi: 10.1650/7356

Milne, H. 1974. Breeding numbers and reproductive rate of eiders at the Sands of Forvie National Nature Reserve, Scotland. Ibis 116:135–152.

Minerals Management Service. 2003. Alaska Annual Studies Plan – Final FY 2004. U.S. Dept. Interior, Alaska Outer Continental Shelf Region, Anchorage, Alaska.

Newton, I. 2003. The Speciation and Biogeography of Birds. Academic Press, San Diego, California, 656 p.

Noel, L.E., S.R. Johnson, G.M. O'Doherty and M.K. Butcher. 2005. Common Eider (*Somateria mollissima v-nigrum*) nest cover and depredation on central Alaskan Beaufort Sea barrier islands. Arctic 58(2):129–136.

O'Reilly, P.T., M.F. Canino, K.M. Bailey and P. Bentzen. 2004. Inverse relationship between F_{ST} and microsatellite polymorphism in the marine fish, walleye pollock (*Theragra chalcogramma*): Implications for resolving weak population structure. Mol. Ecol. 13(7):1799–1814. doi: 10.1111/j.1365-294X.2004.02214.x

Paulus, K.B., and R. Tiedemann. 2003. Ten polymorphic autosomal microsatellite loci for the Eider duck *Somateria mollissima* and their cross-species applicability among waterfowl species (Anatidae). Mol. Ecol. Notes 3(2):250–252. doi: 10.1046/j.1471-8286.2003.00414.x

Pearce, J.M., S.L. Talbot, M.R. Petersen and J.R. Rearick. 2005. Limited genetic differentiation among breeding, molting, and wintering groups of threatened Steller's eider: The role of historic and contemporary factors. Conserv. Genet. 6(5):743–757.

Pearce, J.M., S.L. Talbot, B.J. Pierson, M.R. Petersen,

K.T. Scribner, D.L. Dickson and A. Mosbech. 2004. Lack of spatial genetic structure among nesting and wintering King Eiders. Condor 106(2):229–240. doi: 10.1650/7357

Petersen, M.R., and P.L. Flint. 2002. Population structure of Pacific Common Eiders breeding in Alaska. Condor 104(4):780–787. doi: 10.1650/0010-5422(2002)104[0780:PSOPCE]2.0.CO;2

Posada, D., and K.A. Crandall. 1998. MODELTEST: Testing the model of DNA substitution. Bioinformatics 14(9):817–818. doi: 10.1093/bioinformatics/14.9.817

Pritchard, J.K., M. Stephens and P. Donnelly. 2000. Inference of population structure using multilocus genotype data. Genetics 155(2):945–959.

Raymond, M., and F. Rousset. 1995. GENEPOP (version 1.2): Population genetics software for exact tests and ecumenicism. J. Heredity 86(3):248–249.

Reed, A. 1975. Migration, homing, and mortality of breeding female eiders, *Somateria mollissima dresseri*, of the St. Lawrence Estuary, Quebec. Ornis Scand. 6:41–47.

Rohwer, F.C., and M.G. Anderson. 1988. Female-biased philopatry, monogamy, and the timing of pair formation in migratory waterfowl. Curr. Ornithol. 5:187–221.

Sayler, J.W. 1962. A bow-net trap for ducks. J. Wildl. Manage. 26(2):219–221.

Schamel, D. 1977. Breeding of the Common Eider (*Somateria mollissima*) on the Beaufort Sea coast of Alaska. Condor 79(4):478–485.

Schneider S., D. Roessli and L. Excoffier. 2000. Arlequin ver. 2.0: A software for population genetic data analysis. Genetics and Biometry Laboratory, University of Geneva, Geneva, Switzerland.

Scribner, K.T., M.R. Petersen, R.L. Fields, S.L. Talbot, J.M. Pearce and R.K. Chesser. 2001. Sex-biased gene flow in Spectacled Eiders (Anatidae): Inferences from molecular markers with contracting modes of inheritance. Evolution 55(10):2105–2115.

Scribner, K.T., S.L. Talbot, J.M. Pearce, B.J. Pierson, K.S Bollinger and D.V. Derksen. 2003. Phylogeography of Canada Geese (*Branta canadensis*) in western North America. Auk 120(3):889–907. doi: 10.1642/0004-8038(2003)120[0889:POCGBC]2.0.CO;2

Smallwood, J.A., C. Natale, K. Steenhof, M. Meetz, C.D. Marti, R.J. Melvin, G.R. Bortolotti, R. Robertson, S. Robertson, W.R. Shuford, S.A. Lindemann and B. Tornwall. 1999. Clinal variation in the juvenal plumage of American Kestrels. J. Field Ornithol. 70(3):425–435.

Sokal, R.R., and F.J. Rohlf. 1981. Biometry. Second Edition. W.H. Freeman, New York, New York, 859 p.

Sonsthagen, S.A., S.L. Talbot and C.M. White. 2004. Gene flow and genetic characterization of Northern Goshawks breeding in Utah. Condor 106(4):826–836. doi: 10.1650/7448

Sorenson, M.D., and R.C. Fleischer. 1996. Multiple independent transpositions of mitochondrial DNA control region sequences to the nucleus. Proc. Natl. Acad. Sci. USA 93(26):15239–15243.

Stephens, M., N.J. Smith and P. Donnelly. 2001. A new statistical method for haplotype reconstruction from population data. Am. J. Hum. Genet. 68(4):978–989. doi: 0002-9297/2001/6804-0020$02.00

Storz, J.F., B.A. Payseur and M.W. Nachman. 2004. Genome scans of DNA variability in humans reveal evidence for selective sweeps outside of Africa. Mol. Biol. Evol. 21(9):1800–1811. doi: 10.1093/molbev/msh192

Suydam, R.S., D.L. Dickson, J.B. Fadely and L.T. Quakenbush. 2000. Population declines of King and Common Eiders of the Beaufort Sea. Condor 102(1):219–222. doi: 10.1650/0010-5422(2000)102[0219:PDOKAC]2.0.CO;2

Swennen, C. 1990. Dispersal and migratory movements of eiders *Somateria mollissima* breeding in the Netherlands. Ornis Scand. 21(1):17–27.

Swofford, D.L. 1998. PAUP*: Phylogenetic Analysis Using Parsimony (and Other Methods), Version 4. Sinauer Associates, Inc., Sunderland, Massachusetts.

Tajima, F. 1989. The effect of change in population size on DNA polymorphism. Genetics 123(3):597–601.

Tamura, K., and M. Nei. 1993. Estimation of the number of nucleotide substitutions in the control region of mitochondrial DNA in humans and chimpanzees. Mol. Biol. Evol. 10(3):512–526.

Templeton, A.R., K.A. Crandall and C.F. Sing. 1992. A cladistic analysis of phenotypic associations with haplotypes inferred from restriction endonuclease mapping and DNA sequence data. III. Cladogram estimation. Genetics 132(2):619–633.

Tiedemann, R., and K.G. von Kistowski. 1998. Novel primers for the mitochondrial Control Region and its homologous nuclear pseudogene in the Eider duck *Somateria mollissima*. Anim. Genet. 29(6):468.

Tiedemann, R., K.G. von Kistowski and H. Noer. 1999. On sex-specific dispersal and mating tactics in the Common Eider *Somateria mollissima* as inferred from the genetic structure of breeding colonies. Behaviour 136(9):1145–1155.

Valière, N. 2002. GIMLET: A computer program for analysing genetic individual identification data. Mol. Ecol. Notes 2(3):377–379.

Vitalis, R., K. Dawson, P. Boursot and K. Belkhir. 2003. DetSel 1.0: A computer program to detect markers responding to selection. J. Heredity 94(5):429–431. doi: 10.1093/jhered/esg083

Wakely, J.S., and H.L. Mendall. 1976. Migrational homing and survival of adult female eiders in Maine. J. Wildl. Manag. 40:15–21.

Winker, K., G.R. Graves and M.J. Braun. 2000. Genetic differentiation among populations of a migratory songbird: *Limnothlypis swainsonii*. J. Avian Biol. 31(3):319–328.

Wright, S. 1951. The genetical structure of populations. Ann. Eugen. 15:323–354.

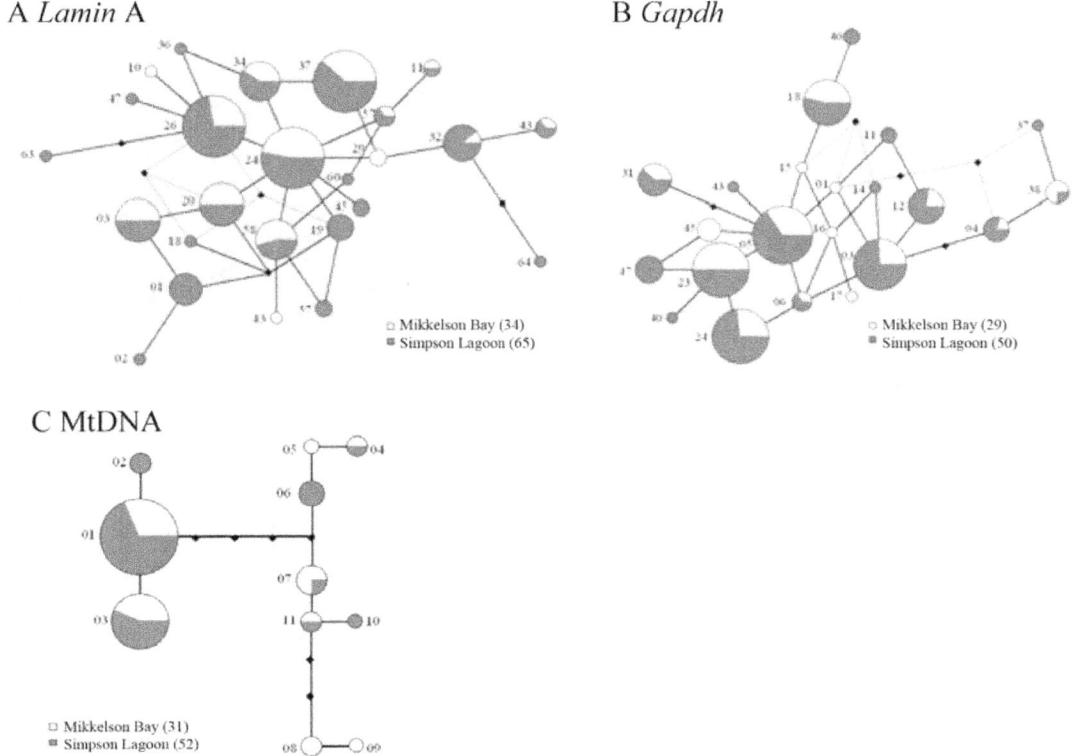

A *Lamin* A

B *Gapdh*

○ Mikkelson Bay (34)
▪ Simpson Lagoon (65)

○ Mikkelson Bay (29)
▪ Simpson Lagoon (50)

C MtDNA

○ Mikkelson Bay (31)
▪ Simpson Lagoon (52)

Figure 1.1: Beaufort Sea barrier islands located in (A) Simpson Lagoon (western group) and (B) Mikkelsen Bay (eastern group) with sample sizes for each island in parentheses, the first value is the number of samples (blood and feather) genotyped at 14 microsatellite loci and the second value is the number of samples (blood) sequenced for mtDNA and two nuclear introns. Wannabe and Camp islands are designations used by the authors and are not official names of islands.

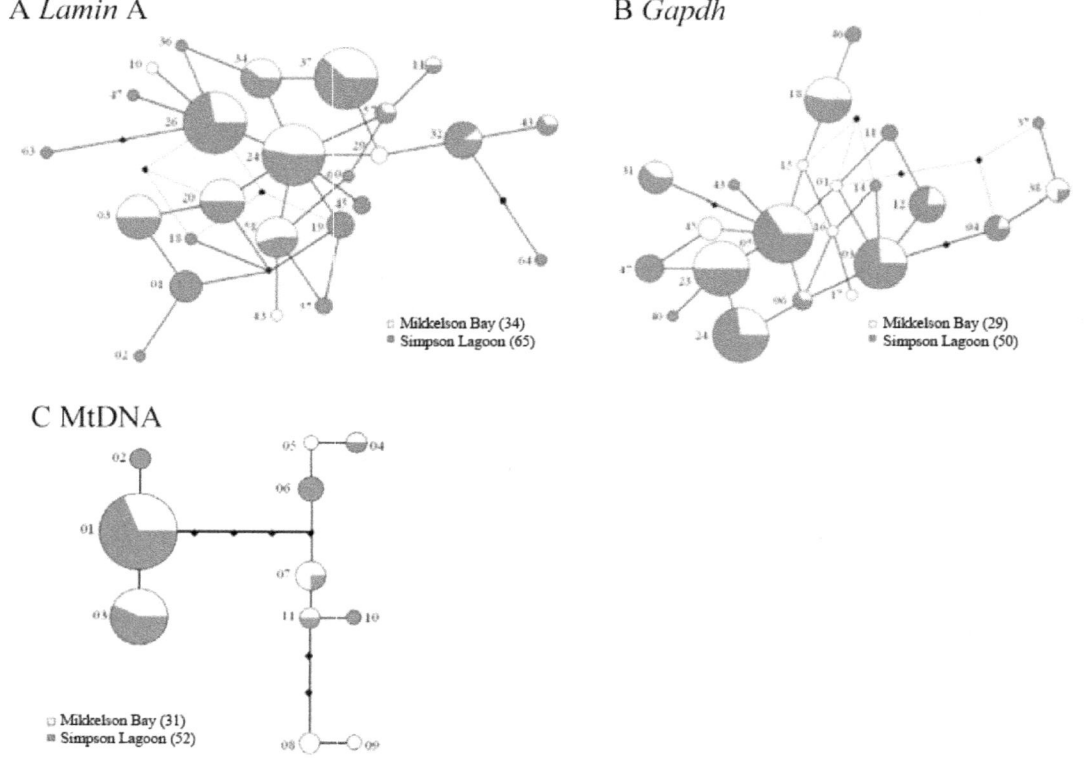

Figure 1.2: Unrooted parsimony tree illustrating relationships of (A) 25 *lamin* A alleles, (B) 22 *gapdh* alleles, and (C) 11 mtDNA control region haplotypes. The 95% probability set of parsimony trees are illustrated with bold branches, with the size of the circle node corresponding to the frequency of each allele. Gray lines indicate alternative branching patterns and possible reticulations. Small black squares indicate intermediate ancestral alleles that were not sampled. Mikkelsen Bay (eastern group) alleles are illustrated in white and Simpson Lagoon (western group) alleles are illustrated in gray. Sample sizes are shown in parentheses.

Table 1.1: Estimates of genetic diversity, including; nucleotide (π) and haplotype (h) diversity (including the standard deviation SD), number of unique haplotypes per population, and sample size (n), for 280 bp of nuclear intron *lamin* A, 387 bp of nuclear intron *gapdh*, and 545 bp of mtDNA control region.

			Mikkelsen Bay		
	Camp	Pt. Thomson	Mary Saches & North Star	Duchess	Challenge & Alaska
Lamin A					
h	0.901	0.864	0.844	0.884	0.600
SD	0.047	0.072	0.103	0.034	0.215
π	0.009	0.006	0.005	0.007	0.005
SD	0.006	0.004	0.004	0.005	0.004
Fu's *Fs* *	−1.503	−2.004	**−2.690**	**−4.704**	0.381
Tajima's *D*	−0.147	−0.212	−0.682	0.226	0.338
No. of alleles	7	6	6	11	3
n	7	6	5	14	3
Gapdh					
h	0.924	0.911	0.927	0.909	0.933
SD	0.058	0.077	0.084	0.037	0.122
π	0.006	0.009	0.007	0.006	0.008
SD	0.004	0.006	0.005	0.004	0.006
Fu's *Fs* *	−1.584	−0.907	−0.930	**−3.602**	−1.466
Tajima's *D*	−0.323	−0.810	−0.856	−0.989	−0.631
No. of alleles	8	7	6	11	5
n	6	5	4	11	3
MtDNA					
h	0.333	0.800	0.400	0.891	0.667
SD	0.215	0.172	0.237	0.063	0.314
π	0.002	0.007	0.001	0.009	0.001
SD	0.002	0.004	0.001	0.005	0.001
Fu's *Fs* *	2.139	0.567	0.090	0.543	0.201
Tajima's *D*	−1.295	−0.516	−0.817	0.591	0.000
No. of haplotypes	2	3	2	6	2
n	6	6	5	11	3

* Significant *P*–values are in bold text; Fu's *Fs* ($P < 0.02$) and Tajima's *D* ($P < 0.05$).

Table 1.1 cont.

		Simpson Lagoon		
		Wannabe &		
	Stump	Egg	Long	Spy
***Lamin* A**				
h	0.849	0.818	0.915	0.876
SD	0.036	0.052	0.027	0.045
π	0.008	0.007	0.009	0.008
SD	0.005	0.004	0.006	0.005
Fu's *Fs* *	−3.499	−3.033	**−4.943**	−1.896
Tajima's *D*	−0.169	−0.126	−0.119	0.070
No. of alleles	12	10	13	8
n	24	13	15	9
Gapdh				
h	0.900	0.874	0.886	0.954
SD	0.024	0.032	0.036	0.047
π	0.006	0.006	0.007	0.007
SD	0.004	0.004	0.004	0.005
Fu's *Fs* *	−2.850	−0.773	−0.996	−2.162
Tajima's *D*	−0.853	−0.836	−0.306	−0.964
No. of alleles	13	8	10	9
n	18	13	13	6
MtDNA				
h	0.579	0.526	0.654	0.000
SD	0.114	0.152	0.106	0.000
π	0.003	0.003	0.003	0.000
SD	0.002	0.002	0.002	0.000
Fu's *Fs* *	0.183	0.868	0.399	–
Tajima's *D*	−0.869	−0.167	−1.249	0.000
No. of haplotypes	5	4	4	1
n	19	13	13	7

* Significant *P*–values are in bold text; Fu's *Fs* ($P < 0.02$) and Tajima's *D* ($P < 0.05$).

Table 1.2: Hierarchical analysis of molecular variance (AMOVA) of allelic and haplotypic frequencies for islands within Mikkelsen Bay and Simpson Lagoon. Significant comparisons are in bold text.

Source of Variation	d.f.	Variance components	% of total variation	Φ	P– value
Microsatellite – F_{ST}					
Variance among group	1	0.003	0.08	0.001	0.247
Variance among pop. within group	10	0.011	0.34	**0.003**	**0.042**
Variance within populations	614	3.251	99.58	**0.004**	**0.016**
Total	625	3.264	–	–	–
Microsatellite – R_{ST}					
Variance among group	1	0.575	0.39	0.004	0.140
Variance among pop. within group	10	–0.106	–0.07	–0.001	0.652
Variance within populations	614	145.949	99.68	0.003	0.449
Total	625	146.418	–	–	–
***Lamin* A**					
Variance among group	1	–0.004	–0.34	–0.003	0.478
Variance among pop. within group	7	0.027	2.50	**0.025**	**0.012**
Variance within populations	193	1.066	97.84	**0.022**	**0.022**
Total	201	1.089	–	–	–
Gapdh					
Variance among group	1	–0.000	–1.00	–0.000	0.685
Variance among pop. within group	7	–0.020	–1.89	–0.019	0.933
Variance within populations	149	1.061	101.90	–0.019	0.929
Total	157	1.042	–	–	–
Mitochondrial DNA					
Variance among group	1	0.000	2.78	0.028	0.202
Variance among pop. within group	7	0.000	5.38	**0.055**	**0.030**
Variance within populations	74	0.002	91.84	**0.082**	**0.047**
Total	82	0.002	–	–	–

Table 1.3: Estimates of pairwise inter-population variance in allelic frequency (Φ_{ST}) values calculated for *lamin* A (above diagonal) and *gapdh* (below diagonal) for Common Eiders from each pair of nine islands breeding in the Beaufort Sea. Significant pairwise comparisons ($\alpha = 0.05$) are in bold text.

Population [a]		Mikkelsen Bay				Simpson Lagoon			
	Camp	Pt. Thomson	Mary Saches & North Star	Duchess	Alaska & Challenge	Stump	Wannabe & Egg	Long	Spy
Camp	–	–0.034	–0.007	0.001	0.088	0.074	0.027	0.026	0.052
Pt. Thomson	–0.027	–	0.034	0.009	**0.173**	0.037	0.059	0.024	**0.089**
Mary Saches & North Star	–0.025	–0.013	–	–0.029	0.119	–0.025	0.003	0.003	0.033
Duchess	0.002	0.026	–0.053	–	0.024	–0.007	–0.002	0.007	0.053
Alaska & Challenge	–0.110	–0.126	–0.056	–0.020	–	0.003	–0.042	0.024	**0.148**
Stump	–0.029	0.024	–0.031	0.023	–0.039	–	–0.012	0.022	**0.092**
Wannabe & Egg	–0.036	–0.032	–0.021	0.000	–0.071	0.002	–	0.025	**0.106**
Long	–0.037	–0.042	–0.040	–0.009	–0.082	0.003	–0.028	–	0.022
Spy	–0.060	–0.059	–0.035	0.002	–0.093	–0.023	–0.054	–0.049	–

[a] Islands are listed East to West.

Table 1.4: Pairwise Φ_{ST} values calculated for 545 bp of mtDNA control region (above diagonal) and *lamin* A site 116 (below diagonal) for Common Eiders breeding from each pair of nine islands breeding in the Beaufort Sea. Significant pairwise comparisons ($\alpha = 0.05$) are in bold text.

Population [a]	Mikkelsen Bay					Simpson Lagoon			
	Camp	Pt. Thomson	Mary Saches & North Star	Duchess	Alaska & Challenge	Stump	Wannabe & Egg	Long	Spy
Camp	—	-0.085	-0.018	0.097	-0.058	-0.083	-0.082	0.000	0.028
Pt. Thomson	—	—	0.032	-0.024	-0.174	-0.024	-0.082	0.026	0.127
Mary Saches & North Star	—	—	—	0.201	-0.299	-0.066	0.040	-0.095	0.073
Duchess	—	—	—	—	0.116	**0.183**	**0.135**	**0.230**	**0.271**
Alaska & Challenge	—	—	—	—	—	-0.141	-0.002	-0.199	0.300
Stump	-0.035	-0.042	-0.051	-0.012	-0.092	—	-0.010	-0.023	0.008
Wannabe & Egg	-0.032	-0.040	-0.050	-0.007	-0.091	-0.024	—	0.037	0.068
Long	0.121	0.102	0.078	**0.205**	-0.006	**0.217**	**0.169**	—	0.029
Spy	**0.208**	**0.182**	**0.151**	**0.330**	**0.053**	**0.352**	**0.284**	-0.086	—

[a] Islands are listed East to West.

Table 1.5: Comparison of alternative models of Common Eider gene flow between Mikkelsen Bay and Simpson Lagoon. Full model migration matrix (allowing all parameters to vary independently) and restricted model (symmetrical gene flow) migration rates calculated from 14 microsatellite loci, *lamin A* and *gapdh*, and mtDNA control region, were evaluated for significance using a log likelihood ratio test. Ninety-five percent confidence intervals are in parentheses.

Marker	Hypothesis	Ln(L)	P–value	Simpson Lagoon to Mikkelsen Bay		Mikkelsen Bay to Simpson Lagoon	
				N_fm or N_em	θ	N_fm or N_em	θ
Microsatellites	Full	−8782.1	<0.001	18.8 (17.8–20.3)	0.683 (0.650–0.717)	27.1 (25.4–29.6)	0.635 (0.612–0.659)
	Restricted	−8888.0		78.3	2.247	78.3	2.247
Nuclear introns	Full	−401.8	<0.001	24.2 (18.6–31.5)	0.003 (0.003–0.004)	34.2 (26.7–43.7)	0.010 (0.009–0.011)
	Restricted	−468.9		22.3	0.006	22.3	0.006
MtDNA	Full	1.9	<0.001	5.1 (0.9–28.1)	0.001 (0.000–0.002)	24.4 (2.4–95.9)	0.006 (0.005–0.015)
	Restricted	−12.0		12.3	0.003	12.3	0.003

Appendix 1.A: Latitude and longitude of Common Eider (*Somateria mollissima*) samples analyzed in this study.**

USA: Alaska, North Slope, Bodfish, Spy Island   70.564°N, 149.895°W
NS27325, NS27441, NS27442, NS27443, NS76480, NS76481, NS76482, NS82136, NS82164, NS82232, NS82234, NS82235, SP001, SP002, SP003, SP017–1, SP035, SP085, SP087, SP088, SP089, SP092, SP093, SP144–2

USA: Alaska, North Slope, Bodfish, Long Island   70.480°N, 148.937°W
LO001, LO002, LO003, LO004, LO008, LO009, LO010, LO011, LO012, LO014, LO017, LO018, LO019, LO020, LO021, LO023, LO141, LO033, LO035, NS82101, NS82109, NS82117, NS82118, NS82119, NS82120, NS82121, NS82122, NS82123, NS82129, NS82130, NS82137, NS82138, NS82153, NS82160, NS82161, NS82162, NS82163

USA: Alaska, North Slope, Bodfish, Egg Island   70.440°N, 148.739°W
EG1, EG10–2, EG2, EG2–2, EG3, EG3–2, EG4, EG5, EG7, EG9, EG9–2, NS76478, NS82102, NS82104, NS82106, NS82107, NS82112, NS82127, NS82141, NS82146, NS82147, NS82151, NS82152, NS82156, NS82157, NS82158, NS82221

USA: Alaska, North Slope, Bodfish, Wannabe Island*   70.437°N, 148.725°W
NS27405, NS27406, NS76487, NS82150, NS82154, WA031, WA127, WA128, WA129, WA130, WA131

USA: Alaska, North Slope, Bodfish, Stump Island   70.419°N, 148.601°W
JAR144, JAR136, NS27321, NS27322, NS27323, NS27324, NS27351, NS27401, NS27402, NS27404, NS27407, NS76483, NS76485, NS76490, NS76491, NS76492, NS76493, NS76494, NS76495, NS76496, NS76497, NS76498, NS76499, NS76500, NS76551, NS76552, NS76553, NS76554, NS76555, NS76556, NS76557, NS76558, NS76559, NS76560, NS82133, NS82134, NS82135, NS82142, NS82143, NS82144, NS82145, NS82165, NS82166, NS82167, NS82168, NS82204, NS82205, NS82207, NS82209, NS82211, NS82224, NS82225, NS82237, ST024–2, ST024

USA: Alaska, North Slope, Flaxman, Challenge Island   70.237°N, 146.640°W
CH116, CH118, CH119, CH121, CH124, CH131, CH201, CH261, NS27280, NS27281, NS27282, NS27286, NS52252, NS52281, NS52282, NS52283, NS52284, NS52285, NS52286

USA: Alaska, North Slope, Flaxman, Alaska Island   70.233°N, 146.559°W
AK132, AK134, AK135, AK136, AK137, AK138, AK139, AK140, AK142, AK143, AK150, AK151, AK240, NS27252, NS27253, NS27260, NS27272, NS27273, NS27279, NS27291, NS27292, NS27293, NS272xx, NS52253, NS52287, NS52288, NS52289, NS76453, NS76471, NS76472

USA: Alaska, North Slope, Flaxman, Duchess Island   70.233°N 146.405°W
DU136, DU210, DU227, JAR136, JAR144, NS24351, NS27251, NS27256, NS27264, NS27274, NS27275, NS27276, NS27277, NS27284, NS27337, NS27338, NS27339, NS27340, NS27351, NS27354, NS27422, NS27423, NS27424, NS27425, NS52256, NS52257, NS52258, NS52259, NS52260, NS52261, NS52262, NS52263, NS52264, NS52265, NS52266, NS52267, NS52268, NS52269, NS52270, NS52271, NS52291

USA: Alaska, North Slope, Flaxman, North Star Island   70.225°N, 146.347°W
JAR204, NS100, NS202, NS203–1, NS204, NS218, NS219, NS220, NS222, NS223, NS27268, NS27269, NS27270, NS27271, NS27278, NS27304, NS27305, NS27336, NS27420, NS52272

USA: Alaska, North Slope, Flaxman, Point Thomson   70.186°N, 146.325°W
NS27341, NS27342, NS27343, NS27344, NS27345, NS27346, NS27417, NS52251, NS52273, NS52274, NS52275, PT102, PT103, PT105, PT109, PT110, PT111, PT114, PT222, PT223, PT225, PT226

USA: Alaska, North Slope, Flaxman, Camp Island*   70.172°N, 146.226°W
CA1–1, CA149, CA150, CA152, CA153, CA156, CA159, CA162, NSCAMP1–1, NS24348, NS27347, NS27348, NS27349, NS27350, NS27418, NS27419, NS52254, NS52255, NS52276, NS52277, NS52278, NS52279, NS52280

USA: Alaska, North Slope, Flaxman, Mary Saches Island   70.200°N, 146.207°W
MS224–2, MS226–2, MS227, MS230–5, MS231, MS233, MS235, MS262, MS303, NS27352, NS52290

* Camp Island and Wannabe Island are not official names of locations on any recognized maps, but were given these names for the purpose of identifying areas in this study.
**Samples are located in non–museum research collections.

Appendix 1.B: Number of haplotypes per sampled island for *lamin* A, *gapdh*, and mtDNA control region.

			Mary Saches &				Wannabe		
	Camp	Pt. Thomson	Northstar	Duchess	Alaska	Stump	& Egg	Long	Spy
Lamin A									
01	–	–	–	–	–	–	–	3	4
02	–	–	–	–	–	1	–	–	–
03	2	1	1	2	–	2	2	1	1
10	–	–	–	1	–	–	–	–	–
11	–	–	–	1	–	–	–	–	1
18	–	–	–	–	–	–	–	1	–
19	–	–	–	–	–	–	1	4	–
20	–	1	1	4	–	4	1	1	–
24	2	4	4	4	4	6	4	2	4
26	2	–	2	7	–	16	14	5	4
28	–	–	–	1	–	1	–	–	1
29	–	–	1	1	–	–	–	–	–
32	–	–	1	–	1	5	3	–	–
34	–	2	–	1	–	2	2	2	–
36	–	–	–	–	1	–	1	–	–
37	3	2	–	5	–	6	5	6	1
43	1	–	–	–	–	2	–	–	–
45	–	–	–	–	–	–	–	2	–
47	–	–	–	–	–	–	–	1	–
56	1	–	–	–	–	–	–	–	–
57	–	–	–	–	–	–	–	–	2
58	3	2	–	1	–	2	3	–	–
60	–	–	–	–	–	1	–	–	–
63	–	–	–	–	–	–	–	1	–
64	–	–	–	–	–	–	–	1	–
n	14	12	10	28	6	48	36	30	18
Gapdh									
01	1	–	–	–	–	–	–	–	–
03	2	–	1	1	1	6	5	2	1
04	1	–	–	–	–	–	–	3	1
05	1	3	–	5	1	6	6	6	1
06	–	–	–	1	–	1	–	0	1
11	–	–	–	–	–	1	–	1	–
12	–	1	–	1	–	2	2	1	2
14	–	–	–	–	–	1	–	–	–

	Camp	Pt. Thomson	Mary Saches & Northstar	Duchess	Alaska	Stump	Wannabe & Egg	Long	Spy
				Number of haplotypes per island					
15	–	–	–	1	–	–	–	–	–
16	1	–	–	–	–	–	–	–	–
17	–	–	–	1	–	–	–	–	–
18	1	1	1	3	1	2	3	2	1
23	3	1	2	4	2	2	5	1	2
24	2	1	1	2	–	6	2	6	2
31	–	1	1	1	–	–	2	2	1
37	–	–	–	–	–	–	1	–	–
38	–	2	–	–	1	1	–	–	–
40	–	–	–	–	–	1	–	–	–
43	–	–	–	–	–	1	–	–	–
45	–	–	2	2	–	–	–	–	–
46	–	–	–	–	–	–	–	2	–
47	–	–	–	–	–	6	–	–	–
n	12	10	8	22	6	36	26	26	12

MtDNA

	Camp	Pt. Thomson	Mary Saches & Northstar	Duchess	Alaska	Stump	Wannabe & Egg	Long	Spy
01	5	3	4	2	2	12	9	7	7
02	–	–	–	–	–	–	1	1	–
03	–	1	1	3	1	4	–	4	–
04	–	–	–	1	–	–	–	1	–
05	–	1	–	–	–	–	–	–	–
06	–	–	–	–	–	1	2	–	–
07	1	–	–	2	–	1	–	–	–
08	–	–	–	2	–	–	–	–	–
09	–	–	–	1	–	–	–	–	–
10	–	–	–	–	–	1	–	–	–
11	–	–	–	–	–	–	1	–	–
n	6	6	5	11	3	19	13	13	7

PART 2: Multilocus Phylogeography and Population Structure of Common Eiders Breeding in North America and Scandinavia

Abstract

We investigated the population genetic structure, subspecies classification, and postglacial colonization of Common Eiders (Somateria mollissima) breeding in North America and Scandinavia and evaluated localities of proposed glacial refugia using microsatellite genotypes, mtDNA control region, and intron sequences from two autosomal nuclear genes. Common Eiders exhibited high levels of structuring at all marker types. Variance in molecular data was better accounted for when populations were grouped by subspecies for nuclear markers, supporting subspecies classifications. Furthermore, populations grouped by subspecies for both principal components analysis and a Bayesian clustering program using microsatellite genotype data. In contrast to nuclear data, mitochondrial DNA (mtDNA) variance was better accounted for when populations were grouped based on geographic proximity indicating a stepwise post-glacial colonization of North America and Scandinavia. Historical population demographic data suggest that Common Eiders were restricted to four glacial refugia during the last glacial maxima; Belcher Islands, Newfoundland, Alaskan North Slope, and Svalbard. Newfoundland, North Slope, and Svalbard localities coincide with previously identified glacial refugia; Beringia (northern Alaskan shelf), Newfoundland Bank, and Spitsbergen Bank, respectively (Ploeger 1968). The Belcher Islands population may have retreated with the Laurentide ice sheet to its present day location. Southern refugia appear to have served as the main source populations for postglacial colonization of Canada, southern Alaska, and Scandinavia by Common Eiders. Beringia (North Slope) contributed little to colonizing deglaciated regions and remain genetically differentiated from southern Alaskan, Canadian, and Scandinavian populations.

Introduction

Pleistocene glacial cycles have influenced genetic diversity and distribution of species breeding in northern latitudes (Hewitt 2004a). Throughout the Arctic, colder climates and ice sheets displaced species to lower latitudes and high latitude ice-free areas during the last glacial maximum (Hewitt 2004a). Fossil and molecular data, however, suggest that some areas of the Arctic, notably Beringia, were unglaciated. Species' ranges contracted into refugia during glacial maxima, and during inter-glacial periods expanded and colonized ice-free areas (Hewitt 2004a). Population expansion from glacial refugia has left predictable genetic patterns in recently colonized regions. Molecular data coupled with coalescent theory have enabled researchers to investigate historical species distribution and demography and identify areas that exhibit a signature of rapid population expansion (Lessa et al. 2004). Conversely, populations that do not exhibit genetic signatures of expansion have aided in the identification and location of glacial refugia.

Despite the importance of glacial refugia in species persistence during glacial maxima and as sources of colonizers of the Arctic, number, locations, and significance of refugia remain largely unknown (Byun et al. 1997, Demboski et al. 1999). Ploeger (1968) provided a comprehensive review of proposed ice-free areas during the last Pleistocene glacial period and postulated the relative importance of ice-free areas as potential refugia for arctic Anatidae based on current species distributions. High arctic ice-free areas proposed by Ploeger (1968) included Beringia, Canadian Arctic Archipelago, northern Greenland, Spitsbergen Bank near Svalbard, and northwest Norway. Proposed temperate ice-free areas included Newfoundland, western Greenland, Iceland, and western Europe. Without fossil evidence, however, it is difficult to determine whether ice-free areas were inhabited by arctic species and contributed to species persistence. More recently, molecular data coupled with coalescent theory have substantiated Beringia, Canadian Arctic Archipelago, and western Greenland as ice-free refugia for arctic vertebrates (Holder et al. 1999; 2000, Fedorov and Stenseth 2002, Fedorov et al. 2003, Flagstad and Røed 2003, Scribner et al. 2003, Waltari and Cook 2005). Convergence in genetic signatures of population expansion among arctic species could provide insights into the locations of proposed refugia and their relative importance as historical reservoirs of species genetic diversity.

In addition to climatic oscillations during the Pleistocene, patterns in the degree of natal, breeding, and winter philopatry also leave varying signatures in molecular markers (Avise 2004). Female natal and breeding philopatry can lead to high levels of spatial genetic subdivision at maternally inherited mitochondrial DNA (mtDNA). Conversely, males dispersing large distances may homogenize gene frequencies among populations at bi-parentally inherited markers present in the nuclear genome (Scribner et al. 2001). If data were collected from just one of these genomes, gene flow among populations might be grossly over or under-estimated depending on which marker type was used (Avise 2004). However, by combining markers with different modes of inheritance and rates of evolution, researchers may ask a wider range of questions involving species population genetic structure and behavior.

Here we investigate the postglacial colonization of North America and Scandinavia and population genetic structure of Common Eiders (*Somateria mollissima*) using microsatellite genotypes, mtDNA control region, and intron sequences from two autosomal nuclear genes. Common Eiders are an arctic-nesting seaduck, composed of 6–7 morphologically distinct subspecies that have a circumpolar distribution (Goudie et al. 2000). As observed in other waterfowl, female Common Eiders are highly philopatric to natal and breeding sites, whereas males disperse among populations that share common wintering grounds. Both sexes, however, display winter site fidelity (Spurr and Milne 1976). Common Eiders are unusual among seaducks, as they exhibit fine scale spatial genetic structuring for both mtDNA and nuclear markers (Tiedemann et al. 1999, Sonsthagen et al. submitted a). High levels of natal, breeding, and winter site philopatry coupled with microgeographic genetic partitioning observed for Common Eiders, enabled us to investigate patterns of population subdivision and gain insight into the locations of potential Pleistocene refugia for Common Eiders and the contribution of refugia to the postglacial colonization of North America and Scandinavia. We evaluated localities that have been proposed as ice-free areas or glacial refugia in other arctic vertebrates and Common Eider, including; the southern edge of the Bering Land Bridge, northern Beringia, High Arctic Canadian Archipelago, Newfoundland, Spitsbergen Bank, and northwest Norway.

We present the first analysis to assess genetic relationships among North American and Scandinavian eiders that uses microsatellite, nuclear intron, and mtDNA loci. The primary goals of this study were threefold. First, we aimed to use a multilocus approach to evaluate subspecies classifications. Second, we evaluated genetic diversity within populations to test for refugial populations and directions of post-glacial colonization. Third, we estimated gene flow among populations within and between subspecies

Methods

Laboratory Techniques

We collected data from 12 microsatellite loci (*Aph*08, *Aph*20, *Aph*23; Maak et al. 2003; *Bca*μ1, *Bca*μ11, *Hhi*μ3; Buchholz et al. 1998; *Sfi*μ10; Libants et al. unpubl. data; *Smo*4, *Smo*7, *Smo*08, *Smo*10, and *Smo*12; Paulus and Tiedemann 2003), mtDNA control region (545–563 bp; Sonsthagen et al. submitted a), 280 base pairs of intron 3 of *lamin* A, and 386–387 base pairs of

intron 11 of *gapdh* (McCracken and Sorenson 2005) from 716 Common Eiders sampled from five subspecies (Fig. 2.1, Appendix 2.A; Sonsthagen et al. submitted a, b): *S. m. v-nigrum* (Alaska and western Canada), *S. m. borealis* (northern Canada and Svalbard, Norway), *S. m. sedentaria* (southern Hudson Bay, Canada), *S. m. dresseri* (eastern Canada), and *S. m. mollissima* (Scandinavia).

Genomic DNA was isolated from blood, feather, or frozen tissues. Methods for DNA extraction, polymerase chain reaction (PCR) amplification, electrophoresis, and cycle sequencing are described in Sonsthagen et al. (submitted a). For quality control purposes, 10% of samples were randomly selected, re-amplified, and genotyped at the 12 microsatellite loci in duplicate. Three primer pairs were used for amplification and sequencing of the mtDNA control region: L263 and H848 (Sonsthagen et al. submitted a), L263rev (5'–CCAAACTGCGCACCTGACATTCC–'3) and H848, and L319 (5'–TGAATGCTCTAAGAYCCAAACTGC–'3) and H848. MtDNA PCR products were sequenced in both directions and assembled using Sequencher 4.1.2 (Gene Codes Corporation, Ann Arbor, MI). Only sequences from the forward strand of the nuclear introns were collected because PCR templates were short (280–387 bp) and sequences had a consistent electropherogram peak high throughout the length of the fragment. Nuclear sequences that contained double-peaks of approximately equal height, indicating the presence of two alleles, were coded with IUPAC degeneracy codes and treated as polymorphisms. Individuals that were heterozygous (48%) for a single one base pair indel occurring in *gapdh* were also sequenced with the reverse strand to obtain data from the entire fragment. Sequences will be deposited in GenBank (http//:www.ncbi.nlm nih.gov) upon publication of the results of this report.

Statistical Analyses

Genetic diversity

Allelic phases for *lamin* A and *gapdh* introns were inferred from diploid sequence data using PHASE 2.0 (parameters: 1,000 burn-in period followed by 1,000 iterations; Stephens et al. 2001), which uses a Bayesian approach to reconstruct haplotypes from genotypic data and allows for recombination and the decay of linkage disequilibrium with distance. The PHASE analysis was repeated three times to ensure consistency across runs. Unrooted phylogenetic trees for each gene were constructed in TCS 1.18 (Clement et al. 2000), which estimates genealogies using 95% statistical parsimony probabilities as defined by Templeton et al. (1992). *Lamin* A and *gapdh* sequences also were analyzed in

NETWORK 4.1.0.8 (Fluxus Technology Ltd. 2004) using the Reduced Median network (Bandelt et al. 1995), to illustrate reticulations in the gene trees due to homoplasy or recombination.

Allelic frequencies, inbreeding coefficient (F_{IS}), and expected and observed heterozygosities for microsatellite, mtDNA, and nuclear intron loci were calculated in GENEPOP 3.1 (Raymond and Rousset 1995). Nucleotide and haplotype diversity for each population was estimated in ARLEQUIN 2.0 (Schneider et al. 2000). Tests of selective neutrality and historical fluctuations in population demography were performed in ARLEQUIN using Fu's Fs (Fu 1997) and Tajima's D (Tajima 1989). Critical significance values of 5% required a P-value below 0.02 for Fu's Fs (Fu 1997).

Population genetic structure

Estimates of inter-population variance in allelic and haplotypic frequencies (F_{ST}, R_{ST}, and Φ_{ST}) were calculated in ARLEQUIN and FSTAT 2.9.3 (Goudet 1995, 2001). Significance levels were adjusted based on 3,000 permutations or Bonferroni correction ($\alpha = 0.05$), respectively. We used MODELTEST 3.06 (Posada and Crandall 1998) and the Akaike Information Criterion (Akaike 1974) to determine the minimum parameter nucleotide substitution model that best fit the mtDNA and intron sequence data. Pairwise genetic distances between unique alleles and haplotypes were calculated in PAUP* (Swofford 1998) for mtDNA and ARLEQUIN for nuclear introns. Chi-square tests were conducted to determine if allele or haplotype groups were associated with a particular locality or region. Hierarchical analyses of molecular variance (AMOVA) were conducted in ARLEQUIN to assess genetic diversity among and within populations grouped based on (1) subspecies classifications (groups: Aleutians, Bodfish, Flaxman, Kent Peninsula, YK Delta; Baffin, Belcher, Hudson Straits, Mansel, Southampton, Svalbard; New Brunswick, Nova Scotia; and Soderskar, Tromsø), and (2) geographic proximity (groups: Aleutians, Bodfish, Flaxman, YK Delta; Baffin, Hudson Straits, Kent Peninsula, Mansel, Southampton; Belcher, New Brunswick, Nova Scotia; and Soderskar, Svalbard, Tromsø) using the nucleotide substitution model that best fit the alleles and haplotypes. Principal components analysis (PCA) was performed on microsatellite genotype data to illustrate overall trends. In addition, Bayesian clustering method implemented by STRUCTURE 2.1 (Pritchard et al. 2000) was used to infer the occurrence of population structure without *a priori* knowledge of putative populations and probabilistically assign individuals to putative populations based on microsatellite allelic frequencies. Data were analyzed using an admixture model assuming correlated frequencies with 10,000 burn-in period, 100,000 Markov chain Monte Carlo iterations, and number of possible populations (K) ranging from 1–13; the analysis was repeated three times to ensure consistency across runs. To determine if more geographically distant population pairs are also more genetically differentiated (isolation by distance), simple Mantel tests were performed in zt 1.0 (Bonnet and Van de Peer 2002). Significance of Pearson correlation coefficients (r) was assessed using a randomization procedure, in which the original value of the statistic was compared to the distribution of a random reallocation of the distance values in one of the matrices (randomization = 10,000).

To assess the relative contributions of refugia for Common Eiders as possible source populations for sampled populations, we conducted hierarchical analyses of variance and grouped populations based on proximity to potential refugia. Given the high level of natal and breeding philopatry reported for female Common Eiders, AMOVAs were conducted on mtDNA haplotype data because gene flow among populations through male mediated dispersal may make it difficult to distinguish between contemporary and historical dispersal among populations. Population groups that maximized the variance among groups (Φ_{CT}) were predicted to indicate source populations for colonized areas.

Historical demography and gene flow

We assessed evidence for historical fluctuations in population demography of Common Eider populations to determine if populations were located in potential refugia. Population growth rates were estimated in BOTTLENECK 1.2.02 (Cornuet and Luikart 1996) for microsatellite loci and FLUCTUATE 1.4 (Kuhner et al. 1995) for sequence data. Bottleneck compares the number of alleles and gene diversity at polymorphic loci under the infinite allele model (IAM; Maruyama and Fuerst 1985), stepwise mutation model (SMM; Ohta and Kimura 1973), and two-phased model of mutation (TPM; Di Rienzo et al. 1994; parameters: 79% SMM, variance 9; Piry et al. 1999, Garza and Williamson 2001). One thousand simulations were performed for each population. Significance was assessed using a Wilcoxon sign-rank test, which determines if the average of standardized differences between observed and expected heterozygosities is significantly different from zero (Cornuet and Luikart 1996). Significant heterozygote deficiency relative to the number of alleles indicates recent population growth, whereas heterozygote excess relative to the number of alleles indicates a recent population bottleneck (Cornuet and Luikart 1996, Luikart 1997). It is important to note that heterozygote deficiency and excess calculated in BOTTLENECK differs from values calculated in other population genetic programs. As mentioned previously, BOTTLENECK compares heterozygote deficiency and excess relative to allelic diversity, not to Hardy-Weinberg equilibrium expectation (Cornuet and Luikart 1996). FLUCTUATE estimates a population growth parameter, g, incorporating coalescence theory (parameters: ten short chains with 200 out of 4,000 sampled trees, and three long chains with 20,000 out of 400,000 sampled trees). Positive values of g indicate population growth over time and negative values indicate population decline. Data were run three times to ensure convergence of parameters across runs. Finally, mismatch distributions of mtDNA haplotype data were calculated in ARLEQUIN to gain further insight into historical population demography. Distributions multimodal in shape indicate a population that is at demographic equilibrium, whereas unimodal distributions suggest that a population has undergone a recent demographic expansion (Rogers and Harpending 1992).

We examined the influence of current and historical processes on population genetic structure by performing a nested clade analysis (NCA) of mtDNA sequence data (Templeton et al. 1995, Templeton 1998). The haplotype network inferred by TCS was used to define nested series of clades according to Crandall and Templeton (1993). Clades were analyzed in GeoDis 2.0 (Posada et al. 2000), and demographic events were inferred based on an inference key (Templeton 1998, Posada and Templeton 2001).

To further assess gene flow among populations, number of migrants per generation (N_em) and number of female migrants per generation (N_fm) were calculated for nuclear microsatellite and intron loci and mtDNA, respectively, in MIGRATE v2.0.6 (Beerli 1998, 2002, Beerli and Felsenstein 1999) among sampled localities. Full models, θ ($4N_e\mu$ or $N_f\mu$) and all pairwise migration parameters were allowed to vary and estimated individually from the data, and were compared to restricted island models for which θ and pairwise migration parameters were equal among populations (symmetrical gene flow). MIGRATE was run using maximum likelihood search parameters; ten short chains (2000 out of 400,000 sampled trees), five long chains (10,000 out of 2,000,000 sampled trees), and five adaptively heated chains (start temperatures 1, 1.5, 3, 6, and 12; swapping interval = 1). Full models were run three times to ensure the convergence of parameter estimates. Restricted models were run once. Alternative models were evaluated for goodness of fit given the data using a log-likelihood ratio test. The resulting statistic from the log likelihood ratio test is equivalent to a χ^2 distribution with the degrees of freedom equal to the difference in the number of parameters estimated in the two models (Beerli and Felsenstein 2001).

Results

Genetic Diversity

Bi-parentally inherited microsatellite loci

The number of alleles at the 12 polymorphic microsatellite loci ranged from 3–49, with an average of 13.8 alleles per locus. The average number of alleles per population ranged from 2.7–9.9. Observed heterozygosity ranged from 44.5–57.7% for each population with an overall heterozygosity of 54.3% (Table 2.1). The inbreeding coefficient (F_{IS}) ranged from -0.005 to 0.445 among sampled sites with an overall value of 0.030. None of the inbreeding coefficients were significantly different from zero ($P > 0.05$).

Bi-parentally inherited nuclear introns

Seventy alleles were reconstructed for *lamin* A from 592 individuals in PHASE with 22 variable sites (Fig. 2.2A, Appendix 2.B). 207 individuals (40%) were homozygous, and 147 (25%) were heterozygous at one site. Probabilities of reconstructed haplotypes for 77% ($n = 184$) of individuals that were heterozygous for more than one site exceeded 0.85, and the probabilities for the remaining individuals ranged from 0.71–0.84 ($n = 30$, 13%), 0.50–0.68 ($n = 23$, 10%) and 0.34 ($n = 1$, 0.4%). The background recombination rate (ρ) was 0.50, with factors exceeding ρ ranging from 0.40–1.94 between 22 variable sites.

For nuclear intron *gapdh*, 48 alleles were reconstructed from 474 individuals with 22 variable sites (Fig. 2.2B, Appendix 2.C). 75 individuals (16%) were homozygous at all variable sites, and 48 (10%) were heterozygous at one site. Probabilities of 77% ($n = 272$) of reconstructed haplotypes that were heterozygous for more than one site exceeded 0.90, and the probabilities for remaining individuals ranged from 0.71–0.87 ($n = 26$, 7%) and 0.43–0.68 ($n = 53$, 15%), which we attribute to potentially high levels of recombination occurring within this locus (0.39–4.41 factors exceeding $\rho = 0.05$, between 22 variable sites). There were two variable sites that exceeded ρ by two or more factors: 2.12 factors between sites 16 and 22, and 4.41 factors between sites 232 and 252.

Haplotype (h) and nucleotide (π) diversity ranged from 0.733–0.901 and 0.005–0.009, respectively for *lamin* A, and 0.506–0.897 and 0.004–0.007, respectively for *gapdh* (Table 2.1). Observed heterozygosity ranged from 32.1–89.2% and 35.3–96.4% for *lamin* A and *gapdh*, respectively (Table 2.1). Significant Fu's *Fs* ($P < 0.02$) were observed for Aleutian Islands, YK Delta, Bodfish, Flaxman, Kent Peninsula, Belcher Islands, New Brunswick, Nova Scotia, Svalbard, Tromsø, and Soderskar (Table 2.1). We did not observe any significant Tajima's D values (Table 2.1).

Maternally inherited mtDNA

Sixty-four unique haplotypes were identified from 456 individuals with 36 variable sites; 78% of variable sites were located within the first 174 bp (e.g., domain I; Marshall and Baker 1997) of mtDNA control region, and 22% of variable sites were located within the remaining 239 bp (central domain and domain II; Fig. 2.2C, Appendix 2.D). Haplotype (h) and nucleotide (π) diversity ranged from 0.230–1.000 and 0.001–0.009, respectively (Table 2.1). Significant Fu's Fs were observed for Baffin Island, Hudson Straits, and Soderskar (Table 2.1). Nova Scotia also had a significant Tajima's D (Table 2.1).

Population Genetic Structure

Bi-parentally inherited microsatellite loci

Overall estimates of population subdivision were significant ($F_{ST} = 0.060$, $P < 0.000$; $R_{ST} = 0.020$, $P = 0.010$). Significant estimates of inter-population variance in microsatellite allelic frequency primarily were observed among but not within subspecies, except among the Aleutian Islands and the other $S.$ $m.$ v-nigrum populations (Table 2.2). Estimates of F_{ST} generally were higher than R_{ST}, with values ranging from 0.021–0.166 and 0.021–0.203, respectively (Table 2.2). AMOVA revealed partitioning among groups, among populations, and within populations (Table 2.3). More variation was accounted for when populations were grouped by subspecies classification rather than by geographic proximity for both F_{ST} and R_{ST} (Table 2.3).

PCA grouped populations by subspecies classification into four clusters with Belcher Islands ($S.$ $m.$ $sedentaria$) grouping with $S.$ $m.$ $dresseri$ (Fig. 2.3). The Bayesian clustering method implemented in STRUCTURE indicated that the likelihood generated for the microsatellite data was maximized when the total number of populations was four (data not shown). Results were similar to the PCA; however, $S.$ $m.$ v-nigrum populations were subdivided into two clusters. $S.$ $m.$ $mollissima$ and $S.$ $m.$ $borealis$ populations clustered together along with $S.$ $m.$ $dresseri$ and $S.$ $m.$ $sedentaria$ populations (Table 2.4). Finally, there was a positive correlation between genetic ($F_{ST}/[1-F_{ST}]$ and $R_{ST}/[1-R_{ST}]$) and geographic distances (F_{ST}; $r = 0.822$, $P = 0.001$, R_{ST}; $r = 0.655$, $P = 0.001$).

Bi-parentally inherited nuclear introns

The nucleotide substitution model that best fit $lamin$ A and $gapdh$ sequence data was the Tamura-Nei (1993) model with an invariant site parameter. Our overall estimate of spatial variance in allelic frequencies (Φ_{ST}) was significant for $lamin$ A and $gapdh$, 0.072 and 0.075, respectively. Moreover, inter-population comparisons (Φ_{ST}) showed moderate levels of genetic differentiation with values ranging from 0.014–0.290 and 0.017–0.220 for $lamin$ A and $gapdh$, respectively (Table 2.2). Inter-population comparisons calculated from $lamin$ A sequence data were lower within subspecies, whereas most significant variances in $gapdh$ allelic frequency occurred between $S.$ $m.$ v-nigrum and all other subspecies (Table 2.2). Alleles in each of the two-allele groups observed for $lamin$ A and $gapdh$ are not equally distributed among populations (Fig. 2.2; $lamin$ A $\chi^2 = 86.9$, d f. = 13, $P < 0.001$; $gapdh$ $\chi^2 = 159.6$, d.f. = 13, $P < 0.001$). More v-nigrum individuals are present in one allele group with the remaining subspecies predominately in the other allele group.

We also calculated F_{ST} values for each of the 22 polymorphic single nucleotide polymorphisms (SNPs). Significant ($P < 0.05$) variance in $lamin$ A allelic frequency occurred at five SNPs; 55 ($F_{ST} = 0.049$), 116 ($F_{ST} = 0.040$), 174 ($F_{ST} = 0.124$), 179 ($F_{ST} = 0.152$), and 195 ($F_{ST} = 0.057$). Significant overall allelic frequency variance was also observed at six SNPs for $gapdh$; 122 ($F_{ST} = 0.131$), 129 ($F_{ST} = 0.050$), 165 ($F_{ST} = 0.151$), 170 ($F_{ST} = 0.058$), 232 ($F_{ST} = 0.122$), and 258 ($F_{ST} = 0.142$). Within $lamin$ A, it does not appear that a single nucleotide position is driving the significant pairwise comparisons observed, and no single SNP accounted for any of the variance observed among populations (data not shown). However, site 258 of $gapdh$ appears to account for discordance among $S.$ $m.$ v-nigrum and the other subspecies as all populations had significant pairwise comparisons except New Brunswick and Mansel Island and accounted for 54.1% of the variance among populations (data not shown). $Gapdh$ sites 122, 165, and 232 are likely driving the differentiation observed between New Brunswick and $S.$ $m.$ v-nigrum populations and accounted for 0.148, 0.064, and 0.082 of the variance among populations, respectively (data not shown). The remaining positions (129 and 170) did not account for any of the variance observed among populations.

AMOVA indicated that variance among groups was better accounted for by $lamin$ A and $gapdh$ when populations were grouped based on subspecies classifications (Table 2.3). There was also a significant positive correlation between genetic ($\Phi_{ST}/[1-\Phi_{ST}]$) and geographic distances assayed using nuclear intron sequence information ($lamin$ A; $r = 0.706$, $P = 0.001$; $gapdh$; $r = 0.791$, $P = 0.001$).

Maternally inherited mtDNA

The nucleotide substitution model that best fit the mtDNA data was the Tamura-Nei (1993) model with an invariant site parameter (substitute rate matrix: R[A–C] = 1.0000, R[A–G] = 31.1491, R[A–T] = 1.0000, R[C–G] = 1.0000, R[C–T] = 32.3007, R[G–T] = 1.0000, P–inv. = 0.9187, A = 0.2248, C = 0.3065, G = 0.1907, T = 0.2780). Our overall estimate of population subdivision was very high (Φ_{ST} = 0.497, P < 0.000), and interpopulation comparisons (Φ_{ST}) ranged from 0.051–0.927 (Table 2.2). Few significant comparisons were observed among the Hudson Bay eiders (Baffin Island, Hudson Straits, Southampton Island, Mansel Island, and Belcher Islands; Table 2.2). Populations that predominately were represented by haplotypes located at the tips of the haplotype network (Aleutian Islands, Bodfish, Flaxman, and Soderskar; Fig. 2.2C), exhibited very high levels of structuring among populations (Table 2.2). Haplotypes in each of the two-haplotype groups observed for mtDNA are not equally distributed among populations (mtDNA χ^2 = 263.6, d.f. = 13, P < 0.001; Fig. 2.2). More Bodfish and Flaxman individuals are present in one haplotype group with the remaining populations predominately in the other haplotype group. There also was a significant positive correlation between genetic ($\Phi_{ST}/[1\text{-}\Phi_{ST}]$) and geographic distances for mtDNA haplotype (r = 0.705, P = 0.001).

In contrast to the nuclear loci, variance among groups in mtDNA haplotypic frequencies was better accounted for when populations were grouped based on geographic proximity rather than subspecies (Table 2.3). Among group variance (Φ_{CT}) was higher when North Slope (Bodfish and Flaxman) populations were grouped together exclusively than groups based on geographic proximity (Table 2.3, 2.5), indicating that the Aleutian Islands and YK Delta populations may be more genetically similar to Canadian populations. Moreover, more of the variation among groups was accounted for when North Slope populations were in one group and all remaining populations were in another group (Table 2.5). Among-group variance was also higher when Tromsø was grouped with New Brunswick and Nova Scotia, indicating Tromsø may be genetically more similar to eastern Canadian than Scandinavian populations.

Historical Demography and Gene Flow

Population fluctuations

Evidence for significant fluctuations in historical population demography was detected based on genotypic data from 12 microsatellite loci. Under the IAM, YK Delta, Bodfish, Flaxman, Nova Scotia, and New Brunswick showed excess heterozygosity suggestive of a population bottleneck (Table 2.6) and is consistent with band and resight data indicating population declines in Alaskan localities (Stehn et al. 1993, Suydam et al. 2000). Population growth, based on heterozygote deficiency, was observed for all populations except Mansel Island, Nova Scotia, and New Brunswick under the SMM (Table 2.6). Heterozygote deficiency was also observed under the TPM for three populations; Southampton Island, Tromsø, and Soderskar (Table 2.6).

Significant population growth based on nuclear intron sequences was detected using FLUCTUATE for most populations except; Mansel Island, Belcher Islands, and Soderskar with *lamin* A, and Baffin Island, Hudson Straits, Svalbard, Tromsø, and Soderskar with *gapdh* (Table 2.6). Theta ($4N_e\mu$) ranged from 0.009–0.138 for *lamin* A and 0.003–0.047 for *gapdh* (Table 2.6).

Populations showing positive growth rates using mtDNA were Aleutian Islands, YK Delta, Kent Peninsula, Baffin Island, Hudson Straits, Southampton Island, Mansel Island, Tromsø, and Soderskar (Table 2.6). Theta ($2N_f\mu$) ranged from 0.004–0.050. Mismatch distributions did not reject the sudden expansion model based on sum of squared deviation statistic, with the exceptions of YK Delta, Kent Peninsula, and New Brunswick. Mismatch distributions did not reject the sudden expansion model based on Harpending's raggedness index for any population (Harpending 1994). Parameter estimates for time of expansion (τ) ranged from 0.497–7.877, with the smallest values observed for Aleutian Islands and Soderskar and larger estimates calculated for Kent Peninsula and the other Alaskan populations (Table 2.6).

Nested clade analysis

Thirteen clades had significant correlations among haplotypes and geography (Fig. 2.4), and NCA inferences for these clades are shown in Table 2.7. Continuous range expansion was supported by two clades; (1) Aleutian Islands/Kent Peninsula to Flaxman, and (2) Tromsø to Baffin Island and Nova Scotia. Three clades (I-4, I-12, II-5; Table 2.7) were indicative of past fragmentation and/or long distance colonization involving all analyzed regions. Restricted gene flow with isolation by distance was supported by four clades (I-10, I-15, II-1, II-2; Table 2.7) and with long distance colonization supported by three clades (I-21, II-3, II-4; Table 2.7) including all populations.

Dispersal

Gene flow among populations was estimated by grouping populations based on geographic proximity and subspecies designation, and among populations that exhibited a genetic signature of population stability, to examine historic and contemporary dispersal among proposed refugial populations. Full models (all parameters allowed to vary independently) had significantly higher ln likelihoods than the restricted island model (symmetric gene flow) across all population groupings and all marker types, indicating asymmetric dispersal among analyzed populations (data not shown).

Gene flow estimates based on microsatellite loci are, in general, higher than estimates based on nuclear intron and mtDNA loci (Table 2.8). Among refugial populations, number of migrants per generation (N_em or N_fm) ranged from 4.53–15.22, 0.27–34.95, and 0.00–3.95 N_em for estimates based on microsatellites, introns, and mtDNA loci, respectively (Table 2.8). Asymmetrical gene flow, as indicated by non-overlapping 95% confidence intervals, was observed among all populations analyzed. Calculations of N_em from nuclear DNA indicated that, on average across generations, more individuals dispersed from Belcher Islands to New Brunswick, North Slope to New Brunswick, and Svalbard to Belcher Islands, New Brunswick, and North Slope (Table 2.8). Most gene flow estimates based on mtDNA control region were low and suggested symmetrical gene flow among populations, with several exceptions. More females dispersed from New Brunswick to North Slope and Svalbard (Table 2.8).

S. m. v-nigrum populations' gene flow estimates ranged from 10.79–25.50, 0.01–85.90, and 0.00–3.17 N_em for estimates based on microsatellites, introns, and mtDNA loci, respectively (Table 2.8). Asymmetrical gene flow was observed among all *S. m. v-nigrum* populations for nuclear loci, with more individuals dispersing from North Slope to Aleutian Islands and Kent Peninsula, and YK Delta to all populations. Directionality of dispersal differed between microsatellite and intron estimates for the Aleutian Islands and Kent Peninsula. Microsatellite-based calculations indicated more individuals dispersed from Kent Peninsula to Aleutian Islands, whereas estimates based on introns suggested the reciprocal (Table 2.8). Gene flow estimates based on mtDNA control region were low and indicated symmetrical gene flow among populations, with two exceptions. More females dispersed from Aleutian Islands to Kent Peninsula, and North Slope to Kent Peninsula (Table 2.8).

Among Central Canadian and Svalbard populations, N_em ranged from 5.47–31.81, 0.00–55.88, and 0.00–41.37 for estimates based on microsatellites, introns, and mtDNA loci, respectively (Table 2.8). Asymmetrical gene flow was observed among all Central Canadian and Svalbard populations for nuclear loci, with more individuals dispersing from Belcher Islands to Baffin, Kent Peninsula to Baffin, Hudson Straits to Baffin, and Kent Peninsula, Southampton to Belcher Islands, and Svalbard to Baffin, Belcher Islands, Hudson Straits, and Kent Peninsula. Directionality of dispersal differed between microsatellite and intron estimates for Baffin, Hudson Straits, and Kent Peninsula, and Southampton. Microsatellite-based calculations indicated more individuals dispersed from Southampton to Baffin, Hudson Straits, and Kent Peninsula. Conversely, estimates based on introns indicated more individuals dispersed from Baffin, Hudson Straits, and Kent Peninsula to Southampton Island (Table 2.8). Gene flow estimates based on mtDNA control region indicated more females dispersed from Hudson Straits to Southampton, and Southampton to Belcher Islands; however, populations have overlapping 95% confidence intervals (Table 2.8).

Gene flow estimates among southern Canadian populations ranged from 7.66–19.26, 3.27–21.35, and 0.21–8.93 N_em for estimates based on microsatellites, introns, and mtDNA loci, respectively (Table 2.8). Asymmetrical gene flow was observed between two populations, more individuals dispersed from Belcher Islands to New Brunswick based on nuclear introns (Table 2.8). Gene flow estimates based on mtDNA control region indicated asymmetrical gene flow among most populations. More females dispersed from New Brunswick to Belcher Islands and Nova Scotia (Table 2.8).

Among Scandinavian populations, N_em ranged from 9.20–24.08, 3.31–15.31, and 0.00–12.96 for estimates based on microsatellites, introns, and mtDNA loci, respectively (Table 2.8). N_em estimates among populations based on nuclear DNA indicated more individuals dispersed from Soderskar to Svalbard and Tromsø, and Svalbard to Tromsø (Table 2.8). Gene flow estimates based on mtDNA are congruent with nuclear DNA estimates, except N_fm estimates between Svalbard and Tromsø have overlapping 95% confidence intervals, but the variances suggest that more individuals are dispersing from Svalbard to Tromsø (Table 2.8).

Discussion

Population Subdivision

Low to moderate levels of spatial genetic structuring observed for bi-parentally inherited nuclear markers were not surprising, due to aspects of Common Eider breeding and wintering biology. Pair formation occurs in coastal waters during non-breeding months, where admixture of several breeding populations of Common Eiders likely occurs. Male eiders follow females back to breeding sites, and males have been reported to have high natal and breeding dispersal distances (Wakely and Mendall 1976, Swennen 1990). Male dispersal, therefore, is expected to homogenize allelic frequencies in the nuclear genome (Scribner et al. 2001). The overall lack of population subdivision observed within subspecies and more significant comparisons between subspecies assayed using microsatellite and nuclear intron loci, supports the hypothesis that male gene flow among populations homogenizes gene frequencies in the nuclear genome, as populations within the same subspecies share common wintering grounds (Ploeger 1968, Tiedemann and Noer 1998, Petersen and Flint 2002). Aleutian Islands were the only locality with significant inter-population comparisons among populations within the same subspecies. We attribute significant comparisons observed to *S. m. v-nigrum* populations wintering in disparate locations in the Bering Sea. Eiders breeding on the Aleutian Islands are believed to be residents, because eiders are observed year-round in near shore waters of the Aleutian chain (M. Petersen pers. comm.). In contrast, eiders from Bodfish, Flaxman, Kent Peninsula, and YK Delta are migratory to varying degrees and winter in the near shore waters of Chukotka Peninsula, Bristol Bay, and Yukon-Kuskokwim Delta (Petersen and Flint 2002, L. Dickson pers. comm.). Eiders from *S. m. v-nigrum* populations likely wintered in different locations over evolutionary time, allowing the accumulation of genetic differences among populations.

Genetic discordance observed among Common Eider populations appears to be driven more by migration rather than mutation, as our overall estimate of subdivision F_{ST} was higher than R_{ST} assayed from 12 microsatellite loci. Furthermore, inter-population variances in allelic frequency were higher, along with more significant comparisons observed for F_{ST} based estimates. Populations could not have been subdivided long enough to accumulate two or more mutational events (Estoup et al. 2002). However, concordance between the rapidly evolving microsatellite loci and the more slowly evolving nuclear intron loci in the lack of population structure within subspecies, suggests that populations have been subdivided long enough for mutations to accumulate. Low levels of contemporary gene flow probably are occurring among populations, despite high winter site philopatry reported for waterfowl (Robertson and Cooke 1999). A *S. m. borealis* male was collected from Point Barrow, Alaska, during fall migration (07 August 1994, University Alaska Museum specimen UAM6631), which is part of the *S. m. v-nigrum* migratory route (Petersen and Flint 2002, L. Dickson pers. comm.). Occasional male dispersal among populations that do not normally share common wintering grounds may provide enough gene flow among wintering areas to limit the accumulation of genetic differences among populations resulting in dispersal playing a larger role in population differentiation, rather than mutation.

Subspecies classifications for the five subspecies represented in this study are strongly supported by nuclear data. Few significant inter-population comparisons were observed within subspecies for both microsatellite and nuclear intron loci based on intra-subspecies comparisons, variance in allelic frequencies among groups, and PCA. Moreover, *S. m. v-nigrum* appears to be well supported by the Bayesian clustering method implemented in STRUCTURE, which assigned a majority of *S. m. v-nigrum* individuals to two of the four clusters almost exclusively. However, *S. m. borealis* and *S. m. mollissima* individuals were grouped in one cluster and *S. m. dresseri* and *S. m. sedentaria* individuals were assigned to another cluster. Groupings could be a result of colonization of populations from the same glacial refugia or contemporary gene flow among populations. Common Eiders breeding in central and eastern Canada and Scandinavia may exhibit low levels of winter site fidelity. In areas where subspecies distributions overlap, individuals may winter in areas that are geographically closer and intermix with another subspecies, rather than migrating farther to winter with populations of the same subspecies. For example, *S. m. borealis* is reported to winter in the coastal waters of northern Norway and Labrador (Ploeger 1968), adjacent to *S. m. mollissima* and *S. m. dresseri* breeding sites. Because there is little overlap among *S. m. v-nigrum* distribution and other subspecies, the split between *S. m. v-nigrum* and the other subspecies would be expected. Therefore, individuals breeding in Canada and Scandinavia may be more likely to intermix with populations of different subspecies, resulting in lower inter-subspecies comparisons.

High spatial genetic structure, assayed for mtDNA control region, support banding data which clearly indicate that female Common Eiders exhibit high natal and breeding philopatry (Goudie et al. 2000). In contrast to microgeographic population subdivision assayed between Alaskan North Slope populations (~90 km apart) and between *S. m. dresseri* populations (~200 km apart), few significant inter-population comparisons were observed between *S. m. borealis* and *S. m. sedentaria* populations. Female dispersal among Hudson Bay populations would be expected to homogenize mtDNA haplotype frequencies. Researchers have hypothesized that if suitable habitat is available, first-time female breeders may nest near their wintering grounds rather than returning to natal sites (Tiedemann et al. 2004). Alternatively, *S. m. borealis* and *S. m. sedentaria* populations could have been recently colonized populations expanding from the same glacial refugium. Given significant positive growth rates observed at nuclear and mtDNA markers, except for Belcher Islands and Svalbard populations, Hudson Bay populations probably were colonized more recently and have not had sufficient time for genetic differences to evolve among populations.

Comparatively higher levels of population subdivision observed in mtDNA relative to nuclear DNA, alternatively could be attributed to lineage sorting. MtDNA has a lower effective population size relative to nuclear DNA; therefore, when mutation rate and selection are held constant, genetic drift has a larger effect on mtDNA than nuclear DNA (Avise 2004), translating to higher estimates of population subdivision (F_{ST}). The effects of lineage sorting and sex-biased differences in philopatry on spatial genetic subdivision; however, are not mutually exclusive and both factors may be playing a role in the degree of population structure observed. However, microsatellite loci have a high rate of mutation relative to mtDNA (Avise 2004); as a result, new mutations are arising more frequently within populations. By chance alone, one would expect new mutations to increase in frequency among isolated populations and, over time, dampen the effects of lineage sorting within microsatellite loci. Given differences in the degree of philopatry in Common Eiders between the sexes and congruence in results between microsatellite and nuclear intron loci, we suggest that differences in estimates of population subdivision probably are more attributable to male biased dispersal and high natal and breeding philopatry in females, rather than lineage sorting for sampled populations.

Differences in the degree of population subdivision observed between mtDNA and nuclear DNA also may be attributable to homoplasy. Not identifying unique alleles because fragments of the same length may have different sequence information, or have mutated back to the ancestral state are issues with fragment analyses (Estoup et al. 2002). Both types of homoplasy could pose problems when assessing population structure based on detecting allelic frequency differences among populations, where not identifying unique alleles among populations may lower population subdivision estimates (Estoup and Cornuet 1999). However, Rousset (1996) showed that there are no simple effects of homoplasy on population differentiation estimators (F_{ST} and R_{ST}) for loci evolving under the stepwise mutation model or an island model of migration. For the mutation process, and therefore homoplasy, to have an effect on estimators of population subdivision, subpopulations need to have different ratios of coalescent times of genes long enough to have two or more mutational events to occur (Estoup et al. 2002). Because our estimate of subdivision for F_{ST} was greater than R_{ST}, mutation, and therefore homoplasy, does not appear to be playing a major role in differentiating populations of Common Eiders.

Phylogeography and Postglacial Colonization

Concordance in allele and haplotype groups among nuclear microsatellite loci, introns, and mtDNA control region sequences suggest that Common Eiders were subdivided into populations occupying at least two long-term glacial refugia during the Pleistocene: *S. m. v-nigrum* (exclusively North Slope populations for mtDNA) and the other four subspecies. The presence of a distinctive northern group suggests a historical split into an arctic refugium northwest of the continental ice sheets and subarctic refugia south of the ice sheets, a pattern identified in mammals by Nadler and Hoffmann (1977). The vicariant event that resulted in the divergence among North Slope populations and the other Alaskan, Canadian, and Scandinavian populations appears to have been maintained through evolutionary time, as few populations share similar haplotypes with the North Slope populations.

Estimates of genetic diversity appear incongruent with demographic analyses, as populations in formerly glaciated regions do not have significantly lower genetic diversity (based overlapping 95% CI) than proposed refugial populations. Populations residing in previously glaciated regions are expected to have lower haplotype diversity due to successive founder events (Hewitt 1996). However, admixture of mtDNA haplotypes from different Pleistocene refugia may have increased genetic diversity of Common Eiders in formerly glaciated areas (Fedorov et al. 1999). Regions where distinct haplotype groups co-occur, such as Kent Peninsula, support admixture of individuals from different arctic and subarctic refugia. Presence of a contact zone between Beringian and eastern Canadian haplotypes in Kent Peninsula provides further evidence for the Mackenzie River suture zone (Hewitt 2004b). Mackenzie River coincides with the eastern and western extent of the North American Cordilleran and Laurentide ice sheets and likely formed an eastern boundary for the Beringian refugium (Hewitt 2004b). Concordance for contact zones in other arctic vertebrates in the Mackenzie River region indicates that this region was a strong geographic barrier limiting dispersal from Beringian populations (e.g. Collared lemming, *Dichrostonyx* ssp., Fedorov and Stenseth 2002; True lemming, *Lemmus* spp., Fedorov et al. 2003; Rock Ptarmigan, *Lagopus mutus*, Holder et al. 1999; 2000). Our data suggest that this region also may have contributed to divergence between eiders from the Alaskan North Slope and eiders inhabiting all other regions.

Historical population demographic data suggest that Common Eiders were restricted to four glacial refugia during the last glacial maxium; Belcher Islands, Newfoundland, North Slope, and Svalbard. Three regions exhibit a signal of a demographically stable population based on mtDNA estimates, North Slope, *S. m. dresseri*, and Svalbard populations, and coincide with previously identified glacial refugia; Beringia (northern Alaskan shelf), Newfoundland Bank, and Spitsbergen Bank, respectively (Ploeger 1968). The proposed location of the Beringian refugium for Common Eiders; however, differs from Ploeger (1968), who hypothesized that Common Eiders where restricted to the southern edge of the Bering Land Bridge. Our data suggest that eiders in this region may have occupied an arctic refugium, north of the land bridge. Moreover, populations sampled from the Aleutian Islands and YK Delta have a genetic signature of relatively recent population expansion, and therefore, it is unlikely that these areas served as refugia for Common Eider populations. Belcher Islands did not exhibit a signal of population growth, despite Hudson Bay being glaciated during the Wisconsin glacial. Given the central position of haplotypes within the mtDNA network representing *S. m. sedentaria* individuals, it is likely that Belcher Island haplotypes are more historic relative to the other sampled haplotypes (Alsos et al. 2005). *S. m. sedentaria* might have been restricted south of the Laurentide ice sheet, as proposed for other arctic vertebrates (Flagstad and Røed 2003, Scribner et al. 2003), and slowly colonized behind the retreating ice sheet to its present day location. Shorter movements from a location south of the ice sheet to present day locations would allow populations to retain genetic diversity because effective population sizes would not be reduced (Hewitt 1996), especially if colonization occurred over a long period. Maintenance of genetic diversity while colonizing recently glaciated areas would, therefore, not be expected to produce a genetic signature of population expansion because this signature assumes low-diversity founder populations (Galbreath and Cook 2004).

Beringian populations (Bodfish and Flaxman) apparently contributed little to the postglacial colonization of North America, as few populations share North Slope haplotypes. Limited post-glacial colonization of unglaciated regions by Beringian populations has been observed in other arctic vertebrates (*Lemmus* ssp., Fedorov et al. 2003). Analyses suggest that Common Eiders dispersed west to Kent Peninsula and northern Hudson Bay, and some long distance dispersal to Scandinavian populations may have occurred. The contact zone between arctic and subarctic refugia in the vicinity of Kent Peninsula may explain why data for eiders in this region do not fit the sudden expansion model, as population subdivision violates the assumption of the sudden expansion model (Marjoram and Donnelley 1994). Surprisingly, few North Slope individuals appear to have dispersed to the Aleutian Island and YK Delta. Minimal dispersal from the Beringian refugium to south-

ern Alaska could be attributed to the longer persistence of the Laurentide ice sheet relative to the Cordilleran ice sheet (Westgate et al. 1987). The presence of the Cordilleran ice sheet may have inhibited colonization of southwest Alaska by Beringian Common Eiders due to the unavailability of habitat and is supported by the relatively late estimated time of population expansion (τ) for the Aleutian Islands.

The central position of southern refugia haplotypes (Belcher Islands and Newfoundland) indicate that populations expanding out of the southern refugia likely colonized formally glaciated areas of Canada, southern Alaska, and Scandinavia. Though the time of divergence (τ) calculated for New Brunswick is recent relative to other populations, mismatch distributions may not be a good estimator of population expansion, as New Brunswick did not fit the sudden expansion model. The Newfoundland populations, in particular, share haplotypes with most sampled sites suggesting this region was a main source for colonizers during glacial retreats through both range expansion and long distance colonization. Low genetic diversity estimates calculated for Nova Scotia may have been caused by a reduction in effective population size through founding events, as peripheral expanding populations are expected to have lower genetic diversity relative to central populations (Nei et al. 1975). Belcher Island haplotypes appear more restricted in their geographic range and this region may have been the main source of colonizers for Hudson Bay and southern Alaska. Slower colonization through short dispersal may have acted as a barrier to colonization (Runck and Cook 2005) of Hudson Bay and southern Alaska by other refugia. Belcher Island and Newfoundland haplotypes are shared with a majority of populations and are located centrally in the mtDNA haplotype network; therefore, these regions were likely important refugia for Common Eider postglacial colonization.

The Spitsbergen Bank (Svalbard) refugium also appears to have played a role in the colonization of glaciated areas in Canada and Scandinavia. The peripheral location of Svalbard haplotypes in the mtDNA haplotype network suggests that this region was not a main source of colonizers for Canadian populations. Svalbard was likely the main colonizer of Soderskar because Soderskar shares few haplotypes with other regions. Shared haplotypes from Canadian and Scandinavian refugia suggest that Tromsø may be a contact zone for these regions. Evidence of ice-free areas in northern Norway during the last glacial is controversial (Ploeger 1968). However, eider relics dating to approximately 115,000 years ago have been identified from northern Norway (Lauritzen et al. 1996). If ice-free areas did occur, this

44

may explain, in part, the distribution of haplotypes observed for Tromsø and the relatively moderate time of divergence estimate. Tromsø could have been colonized initially by the Newfoundland refugium and later came in contact with Svalbard colonizers through range expansion during glacial retreat. Northern Norway has been identified as a contact zone for other vertebrates (*Microtus agrestis*, Jaarola and Searle 2002; *M. oeconomus*, Brunhoff et al. 2003). In addition, Tiedemann et al. (2004) examined the post-glacial colonization of Europe by Common Eiders and hypothesized that Europe was colonized through range expansion by populations expanding from a single refugium located in southern Norway. This scenario is consistent with our findings. Eiders could have colonized southern Norway from the Newfoundland refugium, which was a main source population for the subsequent colonization of Europe during glacial retreat.

Conclusions

High levels of natal and breeding philopatry and winter site fidelity observed in waterfowl have predictable effects on population genetic structure, and researchers characterizing populations using genetic techniques could under- or over-estimate the degree of population genetic differentiation if estimates are based on a single marker type. As seen in Common Eiders, nuclear and mtDNA markers show varying levels of genetic partitioning among breeding sites. Therefore, not utilizing molecular markers with varying modes of heritance could mislead researchers characterizing genetic variation within populations.

Concordance of proposed glacial refugia utilized by Common Eiders with other arctic species indicates that arctic and subarctic refugia northwest and southeast of the ice-sheets, respectively, were important reservoirs of genetic diversity during the Pleistocene. Southern refugia appear to have served as the main source populations for postglacial colonization of Canada, southern Alaska, and Scandinavia as proposed for other vertebrates (Flagstad and Røed 2003, Scribner et al. 2003). Data suggest a stepwise postglacial colonization of North America and Scandinavia by Common Eiders with some bouts of long distance dispersal. Restricted gene flow expanding out from proposed refugia is supported by the increase in genetic differentiation with distance (Kimura and Weiss 1964). In contrast to Common Eiders restricted to southern refugia, eiders residing in Beringia (and those on the North Slope of Alaska in particular) contributed little to colonizing deglaciated regions and remain genetically differentiated from Canadian and Scandinavian populations. Minimal colonization by the Beringian refugium is particularly evident in that geographically

close populations (Aleutian Islands, Kent Peninsula, and YK Delta) share few haplotypes with North Slope Common Eiders and appear to be more genetically similar to central and eastern Canadian populations. Genetic discordance among populations residing in Beringia and other refugia has been maintained through evolutionary time despite contemporary gene flow among populations through male dispersal.

Acknowledgments

Funding was provided by: Minerals Management Service (1435-01-98-CA-309); Coastal Marine Institute, University of Alaska Fairbanks; U. S. Geological Survey; Alaska EPSCoR Graduate Fellowship (NSF EPS-0092040); University of Alaska Foundation Angus Gavin Migratory Bird Research Fund; and BP Exploration (Alaska) Inc. We thank all of the researchers for generously providing samples; B. Barrow, F. Broerman, J.O. Bustness, K. Dickson, L. Dickson, P. Flint, G. Gilchrist, M. Hario, D. Kellet, M. Kilpi, K. Mawhinney, M. Petersen, R. Suydam, P. Tuomi, and University of Alaska Museum, as well as; J. Gust and G.K. Sage, U.S. Geological Survey, who provided laboratory assistance, and C. Monnett and J. Gleason, Minerals Management Service.

The USFWS banding number for the USGS is 20022 and the master permit holder is Dirk Derksen.The IACUC number #02-01 was assigned for this work to Kevin McCrackin.

References

Akaike, H. 1974. A new look at the statistical model identification. IEEE Trans. Automat. Contr. 19(6):716–723.

Alsos, I.G., T. Engelskjøn, L. Gielly, P. Taberlet and C. Brochmann. 2005. Impact of ice ages on circumpolar molecular diversity: Insights from an ecological key species. Mol. Ecol. 14(9):2739–2753. doi:10.1111/j.1365-294X.2005.02621.x

Avise, J.C. 2004. Molecular Markers, Natural History, and Evolution. Second Edition. Sinauer Associates, Inc., Sunderland, Massachusetts.

Bandelt, H.J., P. Forster, B.C. Sykes and M.B. Richards. 1995. Mitochondrial portraits of human populations using median networks. Genetics 141(2):743–753.

Beerli, P. 1998. Estimation of migration rates and population sizes in geographically structured populations, p. 39–53. *In* G.R. Carvalho [ed.], Advances in Molecular Ecology. NATO Science Series: Life

Sciences, Vol. 306. IOS Press, Amsterdam, The Netherlands.

Beerli, P. 2002. LAMARC – Likelihood Analysis with Metropolis Algorithm using Random Coalescence. Available at http://evolution.genetics.washington. edu/lamarc/index html (accessed 7 July 2004).

Beerli, P., and J. Felsenstein. 1999. Maximum-likelihood estimation of migration rates and effective population numbers in two populations using a coalescent approach. Genetics 152(2):763–773.

Beerli, P., and J. Felsenstein. 2001. Maximum likelihood estimation of a migration matrix and effective population sizes in n subpopulations by using a coalescent approach. Proc. Natl. Acad. Sci. USA 98(8):4563–4568. doi: 10.1073/pnas.081068098

Bonnet, E., and Y. Van de Peer. 2002. zt: A software tool for simple and partial Mantel tests. J. Stat. Softw. 7(10):1–12.

Brunhoff, C., K.E. Galbreath, V.B. Fedorov, J.A. Cook and M. Jaarola. 2003. Holarctic phylogeography of the root vole (*Microtus oeconomus*): Implications for late Quaternary biogeography of high latitudes. Mol. Ecol. 12(4):957–968. doi:10.1046/ j.1365-294X.2003.01796.x

Buchholz, W.G., J.M. Pearce, B.J. Pierson and K.T. Scribner. 1998. Dinucleotide repeat polymorphisms in waterfowl (family Anatidae): Characterization of a sex-linked (*Z*-specific) and 14 autosomal loci. Anim. Genet. 29(4):323–325.

Byun, S.A., B.F. Koop and T.E. Reimchen. 1997. North American black bear mtDNA phylogeography: Implications for morphology and the Haida Gwaii glacial refugium controversy. Evolution 51(5):1647–1653.

Clement, M., D. Posada and K.A. Crandall. 2000. TCS: A computer program to estimate gene genealogies. Mol. Ecol. 9(10):1657–1660. doi: 10.1046/j.1365-294x.2000.01020.x

Cornuet, J.M., and G. Luikart. 1996. Description and power analysis of two tests for detecting recent population bottlenecks from allele frequency data. Genetics 144(4):2001–2014.

Crandall, K.A., and A.R. Templeton. 1993. Empirical tests of some predications from coalescent theory with applications to intraspecific phylogeny reconstruction. Genetics 134(3):959–969.

Demboski, J.R., K.D. Stone and J.A. Cook. 1999. Further perspectives on the Haida Gwaii glacial refugium. Evolution 53(6):2008–2012.

Di Rienzo, A., A.C. Peterson, J.C. Garza, A.M. Valdes, M. Slaktin and N.B. Freimer. 1994. Mutational processes of simple-sequence repeat loci in human populations. Proc. Natl. Acad. Sci. USA 91(8):3166–3170.

Estoup, A., and J.-M. Cornuet. 1999. Microsatellite evolution: Inference from population data, p. 49–64. *In* D.B. Goldstein and C. Schlötterer [eds.], Microsatellites: Evolution and Applications. Oxford University Press, Oxford, U.K.

Estoup, A., P. Jarne and J.-M. Cornuet. 2002. Homoplasy and mutation model at microsatellite loci and their consequences for population genetics analysis. Mol. Ecol. 11(9):1591–1604. doi: 10.1046/j.1365-294X.2002.01576.x

Fedorov, V., A. Goropashnaya, G.H. Jarrell and K. Fredga. 1999. Phylogeographic structure and mitochondrial DNA variation in true lemmings (*Lemmus*) from the Eurasian Arctic. Biol. J. Linnean Soc. 66(3)357–371. doi: 10.1006/bijl.1998.0271

Fedorov, V.B., and N.C. Stenseth. 2002. Multiple glacial refugia in the Northern American Arctic: Inference from phylogeography of the collared lemming (*Dicrostonyx groenlandicus*). Proc. R. Soc. B 269(1505):2071–2077. doi: 0.1098/ rspb.2002.2126

Fedorov, V.B., A.V. Goropashnaya, M. Jaarola and J.A. Cook. 2003. Phylogeography of lemmings (*Lemmus*): No evidence for postglacial colonization of Arctic from the Beringian refugium. Mol. Ecol. 12(3):725–731.

Flagstad, Ø., and K.H. Røed. 2003. Refugial origins of reindeer (*Rangifer tarandus* L.) inferred from mitochondrial DNA sequences. Evolution 57(3):658–670.

Fu, Y.X. 1997. Statistical tests of neutrality of mutations against population growth, hitchhiking and background selections. Genetics 147(2):915–925.

Galbreath, K.E., and J.A. Cook. 2004. Genetic consequences of Pleistocene glaciations for the tundra vole (*Microtus oeconomus*) in Beringia. Mol. Ecol. 13(1):135–148. doi:10.1046/j.1365-294X.2004.02026.x

Garza, J.C., and E.G. Williamson. 2001. Detection of reduction in population size using data from microsatellite loci. Mol. Ecol. 10(2):305–318. doi:10.1046/j.1365-294x.2001.01190.x

Goudet, J. 1995. FSTAT (version 1.2): A computer program to calculate F-statistics. J. Heredity 86(6):485–486.

Goudet, J. 2001. FSTAT, a program to estimate and test gene diversities and fixation indices (version 2.9.3.2). Available from http://www2.unil.ch/popgen/softwares/fstat htm (accessed 7 July 2004).

Goudie, R.I., G.J. Robertson and A. Reed. 2000. Common Eider (*Somateria mollissima*), The Birds of North America, No. 546 [A. Poole and F. Gill, eds.]. The Birds of North America, Inc., Philadelphia, Pennsylvania, 32 p.

Harpending, H.C. 1994. Signature of ancient population growth in a low-resolution mitochondrial DNA mismatch distribution. Hum. Biol. 66(4):591–600.

Hewitt, G.M. 1996. Some genetic consequences of ice ages, and their role in divergence and speciation. Biol. J. Linnean Soc. 58(3):247–276.

Hewitt, G.M. 2004a. Genetic consequences of climatic oscillations in the Quaternary. One contribution of 14 to a Discussion Meeting Issue 'The evolutionary legacy of the Ice Ages'. Phil. Trans. R. Soc. B 359(1442):183–195. doi: 10.1098/rstb.2003.1388

Hewitt, G.M. 2004b. The structure of biodiversity – Insights from molecular phylogeography. Front. Zool. 1:4. doi:10.1186/1742-9994-1-4.

Holder, K., R. Montgomerie and V.L. Friessen. 1999. A test of the glacial refugium hypothesis using patterns of mitochondrial and nuclear DNA sequence variation in rock ptarmigan (*Lagopus mutus*). Evolution 53(6):1936–1950.

Holder, K., R. Montgomerie and V.L. Friessen. 2000. Glacial vicariance and historical biogeography of rock ptarmigan (*Lagopus mutus*) in the Bering region. Mol. Ecol. 9(9):1265–1278. doi:10.1046/j.1365-294x.2000.01005.x

Jaarola, M., and J.B. Searle. 2002. Phylogeography of field voles (*Microtus agrestis*) in Eurasia inferred from mitochondrial DNA sequences. Mol. Ecol. 11(12):2613–2621. doi:10.1046/j.1365-294X.2002.01639.x

Kimura, M., and G.H. Weiss. 1964. The stepping stone model of population structure and the decrease of genetic correlation with distance. Genetics 49(4):561–576

Kuhner, M.K., J. Yamato and J. Felsenstein. 1995. Estimating effective population size and mutation rate from sequence data using Metropolis-Hastings sampling. Genetics 140(4):1421–1430.

Lauritzen, S.-E., H. Nese, R.W. Lie, A. Lauritsen and R. Lövlie. 1996. Interstadial/interglacial fauna from Norcemgrotta, Kjøpsvik, north Norway. *In* S.-E. Lauritzen [ed.], Climate Change: The Karst Record. Karst Waters Inst. Spec. Publ. No. 2, Petersburg, Pennsylvania. On CD.

Lessa, E.P., J.A. Cook and J.L. Patton. 2003. Genetic footprints of demographic expansion in North America, but not Amazonia, during the Late Quaternary. Proc. Natl. Acad. Sci. USA 100(18):10331–10334. doi: 10.1073/pnas.1730921100

Luikart, G.H. 1997. Usefulness of molecular markers for detecting population bottlenecks and monitoring genetic change. Ph.D. Dissertation, Univ. Montana, Missoula, Montana, 168 p.

Maak, S., K. Wimmers, S. Weigend and K. Neumann. 2003. Isolation and characterization of 18 microsatellites in the Peking duck (*Anas platyrhynchos*) and their application in other waterfowl species. Mol. Ecol. Notes 3(2):224–227. doi: 10.1046/j.1471-8286.2003.00405.x

Marjoram, P., and P. Donnelly. 1994. Pairwise comparisons of mitochondrial DNA sequences in subdivided populations and implications for early human evolution. Genetics 136(2):673–683.

Marshall, H.D., and A.J. Baker. 1997. Structural conservation and variation in the mitochondrial control region of fringilline finches (*Fringilla* spp.) and in the greenfinch (*Carduelis chloris*). Mol. Biol. Evol. 14(2):173–184.

Maruyama, T., and P.A. Fuerst. 1985. Population bottlenecks and nonequilibrium models in population genetics. II. Number of alleles in a small population that was formed by a recent bottleneck. Genetics 111(3):675–689.

McCracken, K.G., and M.D. Sorenson. 2005. Is homoplasy or lineage sorting the source of incongruent mtDNA and nuclear gene trees in the stiff-tailed ducks (*Nomonyx-Oxyura*)? Syst. Biol. 54(1):35–55. doi: 10.1080/10635150590910249

Nadler, C.F., and R.S. Hoffmann. 1977. Patterns of evolution and migration in the arctic ground squirrel, *Spermophilus parryii* (Richardson). Can. J. Zool. 55(4)748–758.

Nei, M., T. Maruyama and R. Chakraborty. 1975. The bottleneck effect and genetic variability in populations. Evolution 29(1):1–10.

Ohta, T., and M. Kimura. 1973. A model of mutation appropriate to estimate the number of electrophoretically detectable alleles in a finite population. Genetical Res. 22(2):201–204.

Paulus, K.B., and R. Tiedemann. 2003. Ten polymorphic autosomal microsatellite loci for the Eider duck *Somateria mollissima* and their cross-species applicability among waterfowl species (Anatidae). Mol. Ecol. Notes 3(2):250–252. doi: 10.1046/

47

j.1471-8286.2003.00414.x

Petersen, M.R., and P.L. Flint. 2002. Population structure of Pacific Common Eiders breeding in Alaska. Condor 104(4):780–787. doi: 10.1650/0010-5422(2002)104[0780:PSOPCE]2.0.CO;2

Piry, S., G. Luikart and J.-M. Cornuet. 1999. BOTTLENECK: A computer program for detecting recent reductions in the effective population size using allele frequency data. J. Hered. 90(4):502–503.

Ploeger, P.L. 1968. Geographical differentiation in arctic Anatidae as a result of isolation during the last glacial period. Ardea 56:1–159.

Posada, D., and K.A. Crandall. 1998. MODELTEST: Testing the model of DNA substitution. Bioinformatics 14(9):817–818. doi: 10.1093/bioinformatics/14.9.817

Posada, D., K.A. Crandall and A.R. Templeton. 2000. GeoDis: A program for the cladistic nested analysis of the geographical distribution of genetic haplotypes. Mol. Ecol. 9(4):487–488. doi:10.1046/j.1365-294x.2000.00887.x

Posada, D., and A.R. Templeton. 2001. GeoDis inference key for the nested haplotype tree analysis of geographical distances. 11 November 2005. Available at http://darwin.uvigo.es/software/geodis html

Pritchard, J.K., M. Stephens and P. Donnelly. 2000. Inference of population structure using multilocus genotype data. Genetics 155(2):945–959.

Raymond, M., and F. Rousset. 1995. GENEPOP (version 1.2): Population genetics software for exact tests and ecumenicism. J. Heredity 86(3):248–249.

Robertson, G.J., and F. Cooke. 1999. Winter philopatry in migratory waterfowl. Auk 116(1):20–34.

Rogers, A.R., and H. Harpending. 1992. Population growth makes waves in the distribution of pairwise genetic differences. Mol. Biol. Evol. 9(3):552–569.

Rousset, F. 1996. Equilibrium values of measures of population subdivision for stepwise mutation processes. Genetics 142(4):1357–1362.

Runck, A.M., and J.A. Cook. 2005. Postglacial expansion of southern red-backed vole (*Clethrionomys gapperi*) in North America. Mol. Ecol. 14(5):1445–1456. doi:10.1111/j.1365-294X.2005.02501.x

Schneider S., D. Roessli and L. Excoffier. 2000. Arlequin ver. 2.0: A software for population genetic data analysis. Genetics and Biometry Laboratory, University of Geneva, Geneva, Switzerland.

Scribner, K.T., M.R. Petersen, R.L. Fields, S.L. Talbot,

J.M. Pearce and R.K. Chesser. 2001. Sex-biased gene flow in Spectacled Eiders (Anatidae): Inferences from molecular markers with contracting modes of inheritance. Evolution 55(10):2105–2115.

Scribner, K.T., S.L. Talbot, J.M. Pearce, B.J. Pierson, K.S Bollinger and D.V. Derksen. 2003. Phylogeography of Canada Geese (*Branta canadensis*) in western North America. Auk 120(3):889–907. doi: 10.1642/0004-8038(2003)120[0889:POCGBC]2.0.CO;2

Sonsthagen, S.A., S.L. Talbot, R.B. Lanctot, K.T. Scribner and K.G. McCracken. Submitted a. Population genetic structure of Common Eiders (*Somateria mollissima*) breeding in the Beaufort Sea, Alaska. Conserv. Genet.

Sonsthagen, S.A., S.L. Talbot, P. Flint, M. Petersen and K.G. McCracken. Submitted b. Genetic characterization of Common Eiders (*Somateria mollissima*) breeding on the Yukon-Kuskokwim Delta, Alaska. Condor.

Spurr, E., and H. Milne. 1976. Adaptive significance of autumn pair formation in common eider *Somateria mollissima* (L.). Ornis Scand. 7:85–89.

Stehn, R.A., C.P. Dau, B. Conant and W.I. Butler, Jr. 1993. Decline of spectacled eiders nesting in western Alaska. Arctic 46(3):264–277.

Stephens, M., N.J. Smith and P. Donnelly. 2001. A new statistical method for haplotype reconstruction from population data. Am. J. Hum. Genet. 68(4):978–989. doi: 0002-9297/2001/6804-0020$02.00

Suydam, R.S., D.L. Dickson, J.B. Fadely and L.T. Quakenbush. 2000. Population declines of King and Common Eiders of the Beaufort Sea. Condor 102(1):219–222. doi: 10.1650/0010-5422(2000)102[0219:PDOKAC]2.0.CO;2

Swennen, C. 1990. Dispersal and migratory movements of eiders *Somateria mollissima* breeding in the Netherlands. Ornis Scand. 21(1):17–27.

Swofford, D.L. 1998. PAUP*: Phylogenetic Analysis Using Parsimony (and Other Methods), Version 4. Sinauer Associates, Inc., Sunderland, Massachusetts.

Tajima, F. 1989. The effect of change in population size on DNA polymorphism. Genetics 123(3):597–601.

Tamura, K., and M. Nei. 1993. Estimation of the number of nucleotide substitutions in the control region of mitochondrial DNA in humans and chimpanzees. Mol. Biol. Evol. 10(3):512–526.

Templeton, A.R. 1998. Nested clade analyses of phylogeographic data: Testing hypothesis about gene flow and population history. Mol. Ecol. 7(4):381–397. doi:10.1046/j.1365-294x.1998.00308.x

Templeton, A.R., K.A. Crandall and C.F. Sing. 1992. A cladistic analysis of phenotypic associations with haplotypes inferred from restriction endonuclease mapping and DNA sequence data. III. Cladogram estimation. Genetics 132(2):619–633.

Templeton, A.R., E. Routman and C.A. Phillips. 1995. Separating population structure from population history: A cladistic analysis of the geographical distribution of mitochondrial DNA haplotypes in the tiger salamander, *Ambystoma tigrinum*. Genetics 140:767–782.

Tiedemann, R., and H. Noer. 1998. Geographic partitioning of mitochondrial control region and its homologous nuclear pseudogene in the Eider duck *Somateria mollissima*. Heriditas. 128:159–166.

Tiedemann, R., K.B. Paulus, M. Scheer, K.G. von Kistowski, K. Skírnisson, D. Bloch and M. Dam. 2004. Mitochondrial DNA and microsatellite variation in the eider duck (*Somateria mollissima*) indicate stepwise postglacial colonization of Europe and limited current long-distance dispersal. Mol. Ecol. 13(6):1481–1494. doi:10.1111/j.1365-294X.2004.02168.x

Tiedemann, R., K.G. von Kistowski and H. Noer. 1999. On sex-specific dispersal and mating tactics in the Common Eider *Somateria mollissima* as inferred from the genetic structure of breeding colonies. Behaviour 136(9):1145–1155.

Wakely, J.S., and H.L. Mendall. 1976. Migrational homing and survival of adult female eiders in Maine. J. Wildl. Manag. 40:15–21.

Westgate, J.A., D.J. Easterbrook, N.D. Naeser and R.J. Carson . 1987. Lake Tapps tephra: An early Pleistocene stratigraphic marker in Puget Lowland, Washington. Quaternary Res. 28(3):340–355. doi:10.1016/0033-5894(87)90002-0

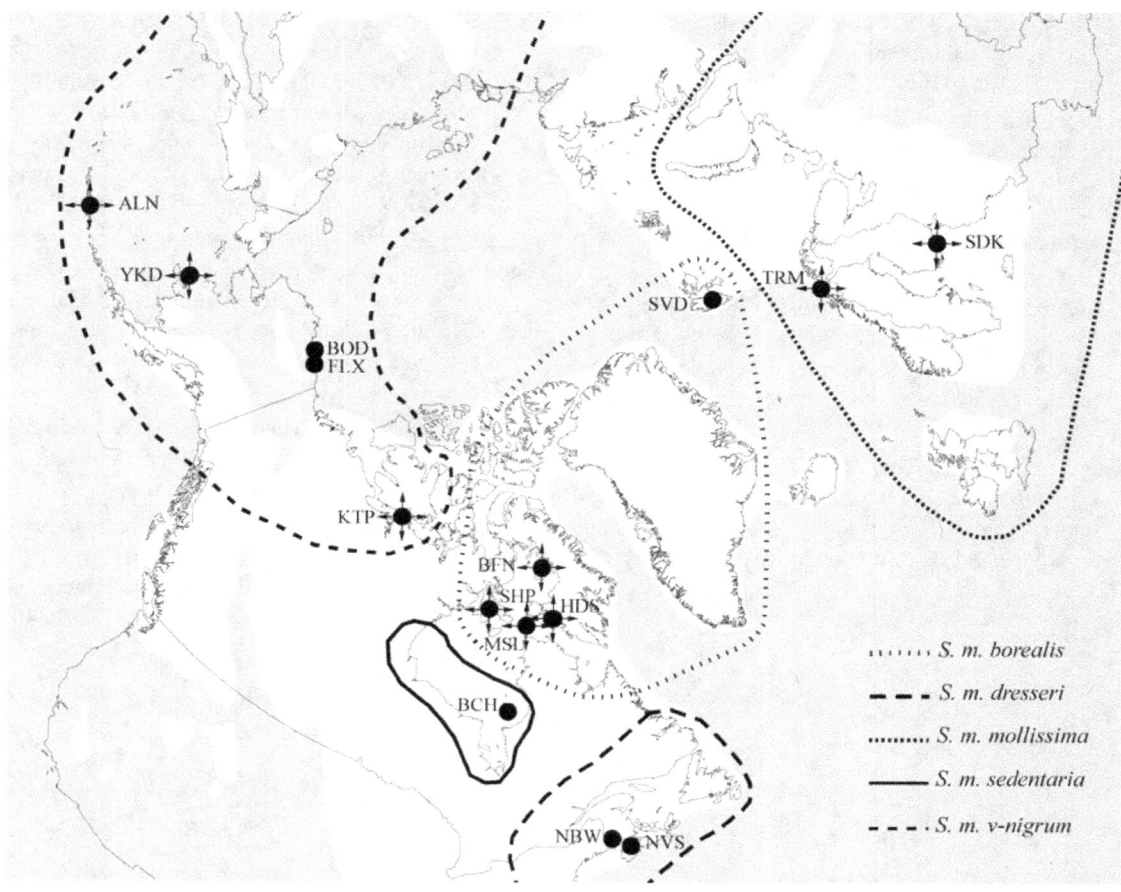

Figure 2.1: Subspecies distribution and localities of the 15 Common Eider populations sampled in this study: *S. m. borealis*; Baffin Island (BFN), Hudson Straits (HDS), Mansel Island (MSL), Southampton Island (SHP), and Svalbard (SVD), *S. m. dresseri*; New Brunswick (NBW), and Nova Scotia (NVS), *S. m. mollissima*; Soderskar (SDK), and Tromsø (TRM), *S. m. sedentaria*; Belcher Islands (BCH), and *S. m. v-nigrum*; Aleutian Islands (ALN), Bodfish (BOD), Flaxman (FLX), Kent Peninsula (KTP), and Yukon-Kuskokwim Delta (YKD). Arrows indicate populations with a positive growth signature. Extent of the most recent last glacial ice sheets are illustrated in white, and unglaciated regions are illustrated in gray (Hewitt 2004b).

A. *lamin* A

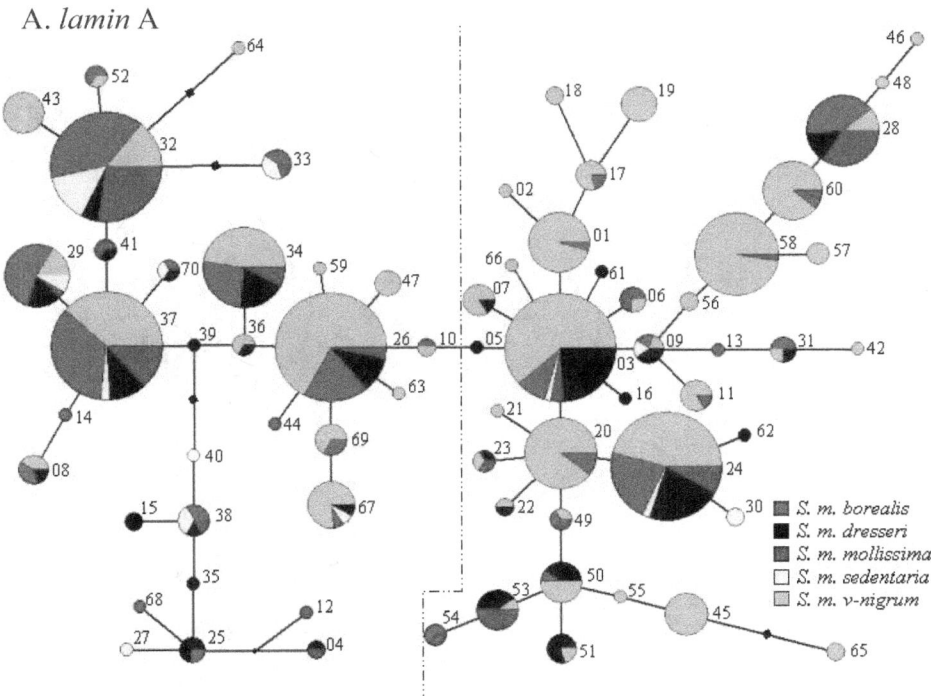

Figure 2.2: Unrooted parsimony trees illustrating relationships of (A) 70 *lamin* A alleles, (B) 48 *gapdh* alleles, and (C) 64 mtDNA control region haplotypes, with the size of the circle node corresponding to the frequency of each allele. Small black squares indicate intermediate ancestral alleles that were not sampled. Each sampled subspecies has a unique color.

Figure 2.2 cont.

B. *gapdh*

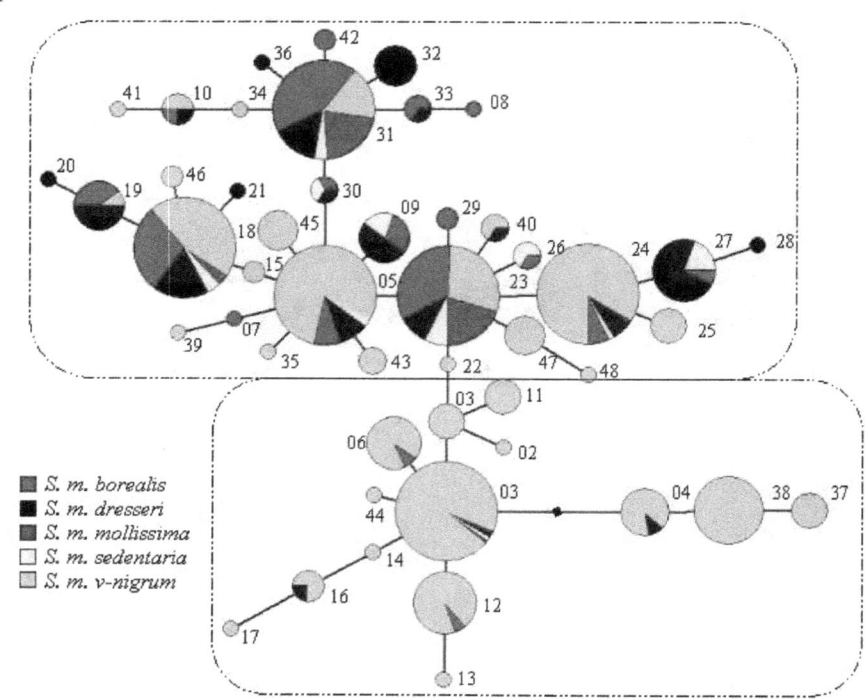

C. mtDNA control region

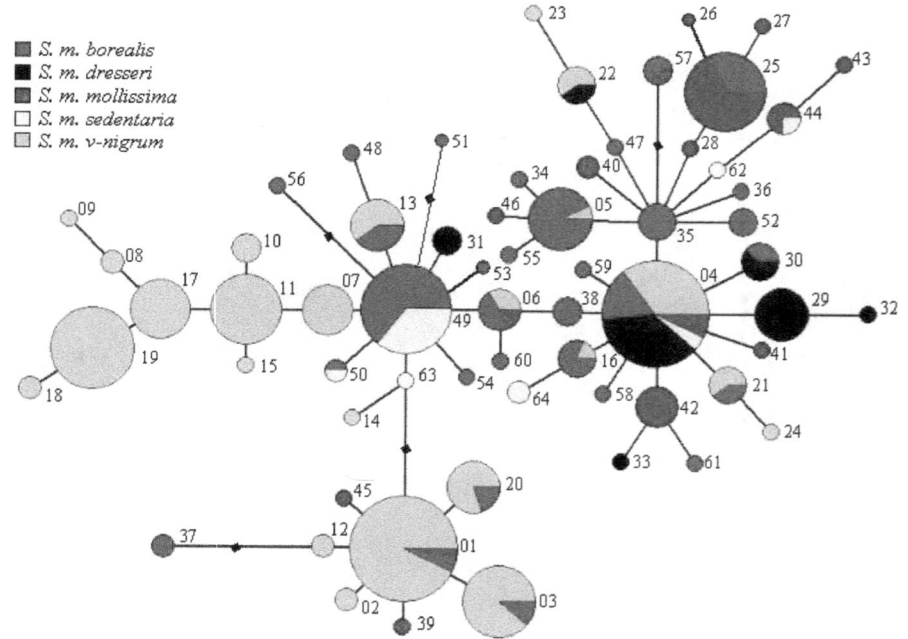

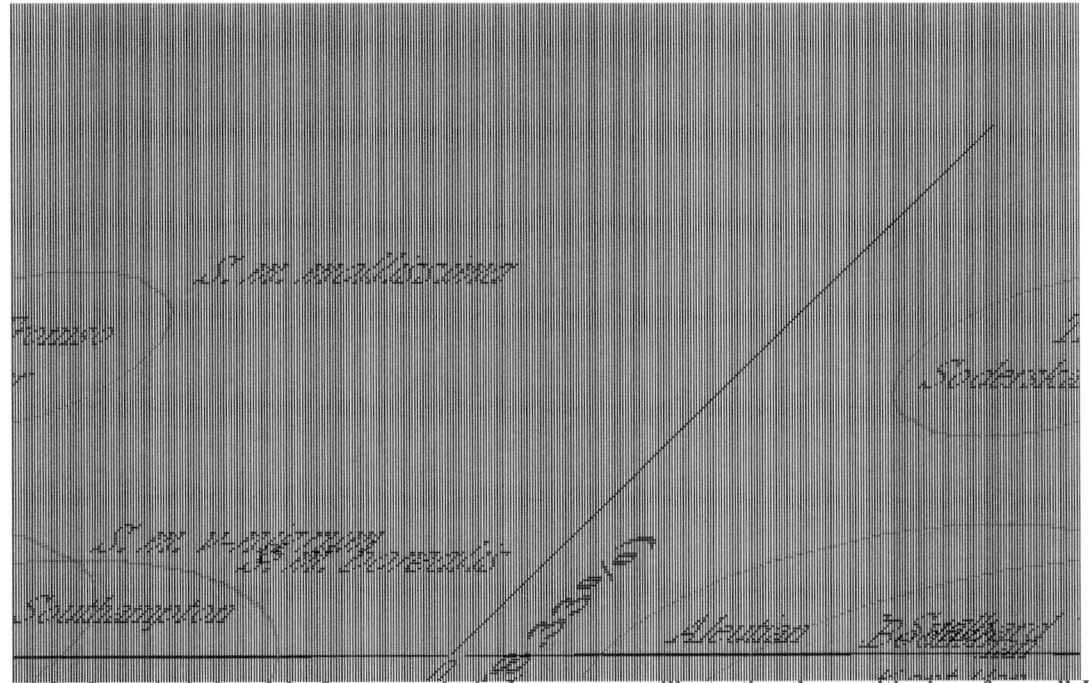

Figure 2.3: Canonical plot of the first two principal components illustrating the partitioning of overall F_{ST} variance among Common Eider populations. Ellipses illustrate the relative positions of populations from each of the five sampled subspecies.

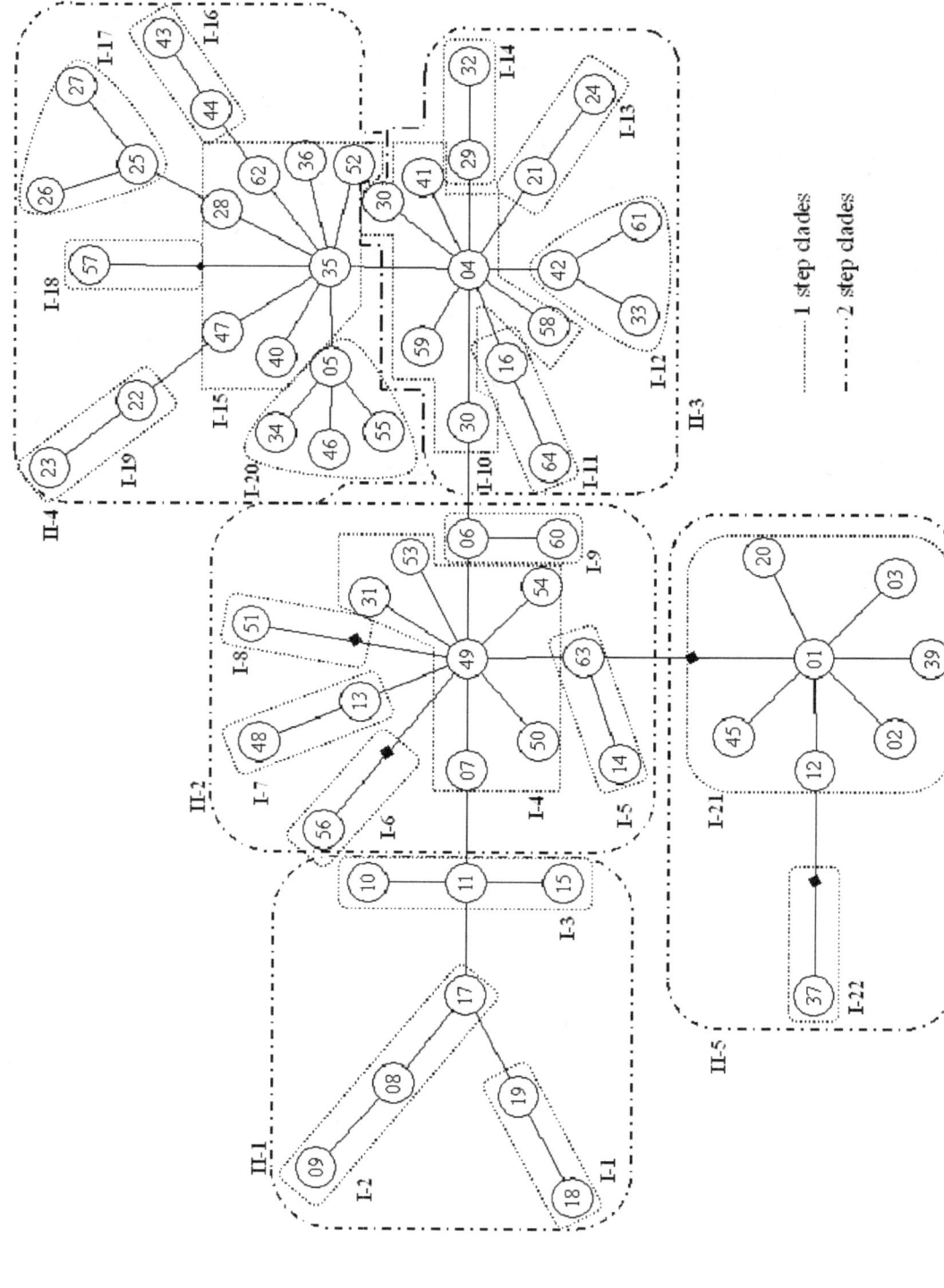

Figure 2.4: MtDNA control region haplotype network and nested design for the nested clade analysis.

Table 2.1: Observed (Ho) and expected heterozygosities (He), haplotype (h) and nucleotide (π) diversity, with standard deviation (SD), mean number of alleles or number of unique haplotypes per population, and sample size (n), for 12 microsatellite loci, *lamin* A, *gapdh*, and mtDNA control region.

	ALN	YKD	BOD	FLX	KTP	BFN	HDS	SHP
Msats								
Ho	0.516	0.577	0.578	0.563	0.549	0.478	0.548	0.535
He	0.537	0.595	0.602	0.587	0.602	0.487	0.540	0.537
Mean no. alleles	6.75	9.50	8.86	8.93	7.43	5.50	6.50	8.33
n	50	124	100	99	41	15	28	52
***Lamin* A**								
Ho	0.804	0.563	0.375	0.487	0.484	0.643	0.321	0.462
He	0.879	0.899	0.871	0.871	0.901	0.870	0.825	0.835
h	0.879	0.899	0.871	0.871	0.901	0.870	0.825	0.835
SD	0.019	0.010	0.019	0.019	0.019	0.039	0.023	0.020
π	0.007	0.008	0.008	0.007	0.009	0.007	0.007	0.007
SD	0.004	0.005	0.005	0.004	0.005	0.005	0.004	0.004
Fu's Fs	**−7.07***	**−18.03***	**−9.91***	**−6.16***	**−6.97***	−3.22	−0.26	−3.92
Tajima's D	−0.43	−0.29	−0.29	−0.26	0.37	0.01	1.32	0.60
No. Alleles	17	31	22	15	17	10	8	14
n	92	220	128	74	62	28	56	104
Gapdh								
Ho	0.918	0.918	0.920	0.931	0.964	0.857	0.900	0.778
He	0.821	0.889	0.897	0.897	0.840	0.773	0.669	0.781
h	0.821	0.889	0.897	0.897	0.840	0.773	0.669	0.781
SD	0.022	0.010	0.013	0.019	0.026	0.052	0.050	0.031
π	0.005	0.007	0.007	0.007	0.006	0.005	0.005	0.006
SD	0.003	0.004	0.004	0.004	0.004	0.003	0.003	0.003
Fu's Fs	**−5.76***	−2.55	−2.74	−2.29	−0.68	0.33	2.51	−0.68
Tajima's D	−0.94	−0.44	−0.48	−0.58	−0.52	1.60	1.37	0.88
No. Alleles	15	21	17	15	12	7	7	13
n	98	170	100	58	56	28	40	72

Table 2.1 cont.

	MSL	SVD	BCH	NBW	NVS	TRM	SDK
Msats							
Ho	0.472	0.500	0.496	0.550	0.519	0.445	0.456
He	0.517	0.481	0.534	0.543	0.538	0.444	0.454
Mean no. alleles	2.67	6.92	6.50	6.50	7.33	5.83	5.75
n	3	37	22	40	40	38	27
***Lamin* A**							
Ho	0.333	0.892	0.400	0.821	0.692	0.730	0.846
He	0.733	0.866	0.782	0.903	0.853	0.861	0.856
h	0.733	0.866	0.782	0.903	0.853	0.861	0.856
SD	0.155	0.020	0.063	0.017	0.030	0.023	0.029
π	0.005	0.007	0.008	0.008	0.007	0.009	0.007
SD	0.004	0.005	0.005	0.005	0.005	0.005	0.005
Fu's Fs	0.46	**−8.89***	**−4.96***	**−11.35***	**−15.87***	**−6.16***	**−5.51***
Tajima's D	0.60	−0.24	−0.20	−0.14	−0.40	−0.05	−0.45
No. Alleles	3	18	13	21	23	17	14
n	6	74	40	78	78	74	52
Gapdh							
Ho	0.667	0.714	0.650	0.879	0.840	0.704	0.353
He	0.733	0.684	0.754	0.886	0.873	0.587	0.506
h	0.733	0.684	0.754	0.886	0.873	0.587	0.506
SD	0.155	0.056	0.065	0.016	0.028	0.048	0.069
π	0.006	0.005	0.005	0.007	0.006	0.005	0.004
SD	0.004	0.003	0.003	0.004	0.004	0.003	0.003
Fu's Fs	1.31	−0.48	−2.57	−1.41	−3.39	1.57	3.13
Tajima's D	0.37	−0.12	0.28	0.87	−0.40	0.71	0.72
No. Alleles	3	9	10	14	14	6	3
n	6	56	40	66	50	56	34

Table 2.1 cont.

	MSL	SVD	BCH	NBW	NVS	TRM	SDK
MtDNA							
h	1.000	0.900	0.726	0.714	0.230	0.877	0.380
SD	0.272	0.032	0.092	0.058	0.110	0.043	0.134
π	0.004	0.006	0.004	0.003	0.001	0.006	0.001
SD	0.003	0.003	0.003	0.002	0.001	0.003	0.001
Fu's Fs	−0.69	−2.54	−0.81	−0.22	−1.46	−3.76	**−2.07***
Tajima's D	0.00	−0.31	0.04	−0.89	**−2.09***	−0.38	−1.42
No. haplotypes	3	11	7	6	4	12	4
n	3	27	20	31	25	26	19

Table 2.2: Pairwise F_{ST}, R_{ST}, and Φ_{ST} values for 12 microsatellite loci, *lamin* A, *gapdh*, and mtDNA control region for 15 Common Eider populations. Significant pairwise comparisons ($\alpha = 0.05$) are in bold text, and populations representing the same subspecies are shaded in gray.

	Msat–F_{ST}	Msat–R_{ST}	*Lamin* A	*Gapdh*	MtDNA
Aleutians vs.					
—YK Delta	**0.021**	**0.018**	**0.027**	**0.019**	**0.580**
—Bodfish	**0.024**	0.019	**0.049**	0.012	**0.820**
—Flaxman	**0.025**	0.007	**0.028**	**0.017**	**0.677**
—Kent Pen.	**0.029**	0.021	**0.034**	**0.032**	**0.610**
—Baffin	**0.085**	0.017	**0.207**	**0.119**	**0.819**
—Hudson Straits	**0.067**	**0.050**	**0.165**	**0.199**	**0.749**
—Southampton	**0.069**	0.006	**0.158**	**0.128**	**0.718**
—Mansel Is.	**0.092**	**0.195**	**0.290**	0.097	**0.823**
—Svalbard	**0.088**	0.014	**0.108**	**0.095**	**0.758**
—Belcher	**0.088**	**0.085**	**0.285**	**0.087**	**0.797**
—New Brunswick	**0.062**	0.015	**0.054**	**0.154**	**0.848**
—Nova Scotia	**0.050**	0.022	**0.049**	**0.107**	**0.892**
—Tromsø	**0.122**	**0.050**	**0.127**	**0.138**	**0.760**
—Soderskar	**0.148**	**0.123**	**0.208**	**0.135**	**0.927**
YK Delta vs.					
—Bodfish	0.002	0.007	0.006	0.000	**0.579**
—Flaxman	0.001	−0.008	0.001	0.002	**0.424**
—Kent Pen.	0.003	−0.007	0.004	−0.005	**0.185**
—Baffin	**0.090**	**0.043**	**0.158**	**0.093**	**0.146**
—Hudson Straits	**0.068**	0.028	**0.095**	**0.170**	**0.142**
—Southampton	**0.072**	0.000	**0.095**	**0.110**	**0.121**
—Mansel Is.	**0.096**	0.046	**0.206**	0.066	**0.308**
—Svalbard	**0.098**	0.034	**0.081**	**0.103**	**0.204**
—Belcher	**0.083**	**0.046**	**0.224**	**0.105**	**0.173**
—New Brunswick	**0.061**	0.003	**0.015**	**0.129**	**0.246**
—Nova Scotia	**0.056**	0.020	**0.020**	**0.081**	**0.256**
—Tromsø	**0.132**	**0.086**	**0.088**	**0.139**	**0.155**
—Soderskar	**0.145**	**0.135**	**0.154**	**0.143**	**0.573**
Bodfish vs.					
—Flaxman	0.001	0.000	0.000	−0.005	**0.051**
—Kent Pen.	0.001	0.003	0.005	0.001	**0.300**
—Baffin	**0.091**	**0.032**	**0.141**	**0.085**	**0.714**
—Hudson Straits	**0.067**	0.009	**0.071**	**0.173**	**0.545**
—Southampton	**0.073**	0.006	**0.070**	**0.109**	**0.532**
—Mansel Is.	0.102	−0.055	**0.187**	0.058	**0.637**
—Svalbard	**0.100**	0.024	**0.071**	**0.092**	**0.623**
—Belcher	**0.084**	0.018	**0.209**	**0.090**	**0.626**
—New Brunswick	**0.060**	0.009	**0.014**	**0.122**	**0.771**

Table 2.2 cont

	Msat–F_{ST}	Msat–R_{ST}	Lamin A	Gapdh	MtDNA
—Nova Scotia	0.058	0.017	0.027	0.072	0.827
—Tromsø	0.134	0.045	0.079	0.134	0.654
—Soderskar	0.145	0.057	0.141	0.134	0.851
Flaxman vs.					
—Kent Pen.	0.002	–0.008	–0.004	0.002	0.155
—Baffin	0.102	0.021	0.170	0.055	0.514
—Hudson Straits	0.077	0.001	0.088	0.158	0.331
—Southampton	0.082	–0.005	0.082	0.086	0.361
—Mansel Is.	0.110	–0.052	0.245	0.031	0.304
—Svalbard	0.107	0.013	0.073	0.074	0.453
—Belcher	0.091	0.010	0.246	0.076	0.406
—New Brunswick	0.069	–0.003	0.004	0.094	0.633
—Nova Scotia	0.061	0.004	0.012	0.043	0.690
—Tromsø	0.146	0.040	0.086	0.123	0.486
—Soderskar	0.159	0.058	0.160	0.124	0.725
Kent Pen. vs.					
—Baffin	0.096	0.051	0.143	0.114	0.180
—Hudson Straits	0.076	0.034	0.070	0.220	0.071
—Southampton	0.082	0.000	0.068	0.139	0.091
—Mansel Is.	0.106	0.034	0.180	0.109	0.086
—Svalbard	0.111	0.040	0.059	0.134	0.153
—Belcher	0.081	0.047	0.210	0.137	0.150
—New Brunswick	0.073	0.006	0.009	0.141	0.330
—Nova Scotia	0.067	0.025	0.016	0.084	0.377
—Tromsø	0.157	0.095	0.062	0.186	0.185
—Soderskar	0.166	0.142	0.135	0.195	0.506
Baffin Is. vs.					
—Hudson Straits	0.000	0.006	0.038	0.037	0.079
—Southampton	0.011	0.015	0.051	–0.012	0.036
—Mansel Is.	0.024	0.148	–0.035	–0.096	0.410
—Svalbard	0.017	–0.010	0.053	–0.004	0.019
—Belcher	0.014	0.044	–0.008	0.013	0.131
—New Brunswick	0.041	0.026	0.124	–0.014	0.153
—Nova Scotia	0.037	0.013	0.127	–0.012	0.242
—Tromsø	0.061	0.001	0.030	0.023	0.006
—Soderskar	0.061	0.035	0.029	0.030	0.597
Hudson Straits vs.					
—Southampton	0.001	0.010	–0.010	0.005	–0.013
—Mansel Is.	0.006	0.027	0.014	–0.076	0.122
—Svalbard	0.004	0.002	0.034	0.041	0.044
—Belcher	0.015	–0.015	0.078	0.092	0.017
—New Brunswick	0.026	0.008	0.060	0.031	0.290

Table 2.2 cont

	Msat–F_{ST}	Msat–R_{ST}	Lamin A	Gapdh	MtDNA
—Nova Scotia	**0.023**	0.003	**0.065**	**0.100**	**0.403**
—Tromsø	**0.036**	0.030	0.016	0.003	**0.099**
—Soderskar	0.039	0.040	**0.036**	0.024	**0.547**
Southampton Is. vs.					
—Mansel Is.	0.012	0.089	0.044	−0.092	0.165
—Svalbard	0.004	0.008	**0.039**	0.010	**0.043**
—Belcher	**0.029**	**0.039**	0.104	0.039	0.022
—New Brunswick	**0.030**	−0.004	**0.059**	0.002	**0.192**
—Nova Scotia	**0.026**	0.011	**0.062**	0.029	0.253
—Tromsø	**0.024**	**0.052**	**0.030**	0.009	**0.060**
—Soderskar	0.033	**0.099**	**0.049**	0.022	**0.476**
Mansel Is. vs.					
—Svalbard	0.004	0.129	0.064	−0.083	0.272
—Belcher	0.015	−0.039	−0.067	−0.047	0.152
—New Brunswick	0.027	0.047	**0.176**	−0.078	**0.626**
—Nova Scotia	0.022	0.084	**0.183**	−0.041	**0.851**
—Tromsø	0.031	**0.199**	0.007	−0.084	**0.359**
—Soderskar	0.029	**0.203**	−0.016	−0.074	**0.888**
Svalbard vs.					
—Belcher	**0.029**	0.032	**0.108**	−0.010	**0.132**
—New Brunswick	0.041	0.016	**0.051**	0.027	**0.239**
—Nova Scotia	0.028	0.003	**0.044**	0.035	**0.300**
—Tromsø	0.014	0.005	0.003	0.000	**0.053**
—Soderskar	0.021	**0.040**	**0.025**	−0.008	**0.333**
Belcher Is. vs.					
—New Brunswick	**0.035**	**0.024**	**0.194**	**0.046**	**0.337**
—Nova Scotia	**0.025**	0.014	**0.197**	**0.037**	**0.485**
—Tromsø	**0.075**	**0.066**	**0.064**	0.025	**0.140**
—Soderskar	**0.071**	**0.063**	**0.054**	0.009	**0.655**
New Brunswick vs.					
—Nova Scotia	0.002	−0.002	−0.004	0.009	0.077
—Tromsø	**0.079**	**0.064**	**0.063**	**0.038**	**0.131**
—Soderskar	**0.086**	**0.112**	**0.109**	**0.050**	**0.690**
Nova Scotia vs.					
—Tromsø	**0.065**	**0.039**	**0.057**	**0.082**	**0.143**
—Soderskar	**0.071**	**0.076**	**0.109**	**0.088**	**0.860**
Tromsø vs.					
—Soderskar	0.006	0.007	**0.030**	−0.019	**0.495**

Table 2.3: Hierarchical analysis of molecular variance (AMOVA) of allelic and haplotypic frequencies for populations classified by (1) subspecies and (2) geographic proximity. Significant comparisons are in bold text.

Source of Variation	d.f.	Variance components	% total variation	Φ	P-value
Grouped by Subspecies					
Microsatellite – F_{ST}					
Variance among ssp.	3	0.275	7.66	**0.077**	**≤ 0.001**
Variance among pop. within ssp.	11	0.027	0.75	**0.008**	**≤ 0.001**
Variance within populations	1415	3.295	91.60	**0.084**	**≤ 0.001**
Total	1429	3.597	–	–	–
Microsatellite – R_{ST}					
Variance among ssp.	3	6.476	2.62	**0.026**	**≤ 0.001**
Variance among pop. within ssp.	11	0.702	0.28	**0.003**	**≤ 0.001**
Variance within populations	1415	240.340	97.10	**0.029**	**≤ 0.001**
Total	1429	247.572	–	–	–
Lamin A					
Variance among ssp.	3	0.629	5.21	**0.052**	**≤ 0.001**
Variance among pop. within ssp.	11	0.040	3.27	**0.035**	**≤ 0.001**
Variance within populations	1151	1.105	91.52	**0.085**	**≤ 0.001**
Total	1165	1.208	–	–	–
Gapdh					
Variance among ssp.	3	0.099	9.20	**0.092**	**≤ 0.001**
Variance among pop. within ssp.	11	0.009	0.79	**0.009**	**≤ 0.001**
Variance within populations	913	0.970	90.01	**0.100**	**≤ 0.001**
Total	927	1.078	–	–	–
Mitochondrial DNA					
Variance among ssp.	3	0.001	16.60	**0.166**	**≤ 0.001**
Variance among pop. within ssp.	11	0.002	35.42	**0.425**	**≤ 0.001**
Variance within populations	435	0.002	47.99	**0.520**	**≤ 0.001**
Total	449	0.005	–	–	–

Table 2.3 cont.

Source of Variation	d.f.	Variance components	% total variation	Φ	P-value
Grouped by Geographic Proximity					
Microsatellite – F_{ST}					
Variance among region	3	0.206	5.78	**0.058**	**≤ 0.001**
Variance among pop. within region	11	0.063	1.78	**0.019**	**≤ 0.001**
Variance within populations	1415	3.295	92.45	0.076	**≤ 0.001**
Total	1429	3.564	–	–	–
Microsatellite – R_{ST}					
Variance among region	3	4.719	1.91	**0.019**	**≤ 0.001**
Variance among pop. within region	11	1.648	0.67	**0.007**	**≤ 0.001**
Variance within populations	1415	240.340	97.42	0.026	**≤ 0.001**
Total	1429	246.706	–	–	–
Lamin A					
Variance among region	3	0.066	5.44	**0.054**	**≤ 0.001**
Variance among pop. within region	11	0.035	2.93	**0.031**	**≤ 0.001**
Variance within populations	1151	1.105	91.63	0.084	**≤ 0.001**
Total	1165	1.206	–	–	–
Gapdh					
Variance among region	3	0.068	6.37	**0.064**	**≤ 0.001**
Variance among pop. within region	11	0.028	2.63	**0.028**	**≤ 0.001**
Variance within populations	913	0.971	91.00	0.090	**≤ 0.001**
Total	927	1.066	–	–	–
Mitochondrial DNA					
Variance among region	3	0.001	17.86	**0.179**	**≤ 0.001**
Variance among pop. within region	11	0.002	34.03	**0.414**	**≤ 0.001**
Variance within populations	435	0.002	48.10	**0.519**	**≤ 0.001**
Total	449	0.005	–	–	–

Table 2.4: Proportion of individuals from sampled populations in each of the four clusters inferred from 12 microsatellite loci in STRUCTURE (Pritchard et al. 2000).

Population	Inferred Cluster				n
	1	2	3	4	
ALN	0.069	0.591	0.211	0.129	48
YKD	0.039	0.424	0.442	0.095	124
BOD	0.033	0.385	0.483	0.099	100
FLX	0.039	0.411	0.470	0.080	99
KTP	0.031	0.379	0.476	0.114	41
BFN	0.528	0.094	0.111	0.267	15
HDS	0.536	0.062	0.056	0.346	28
SHP	0.617	0.068	0.047	0.269	52
MSL	0.757	0.030	0.026	0.188	3
SVD	0.677	0.036	0.058	0.228	37
BCH	0.344	0.051	0.047	0.557	22
NBW	0.159	0.072	0.049	0.721	40
NVS	0.172	0.062	0.058	0.708	40
TRM	0.867	0.022	0.021	0.090	38
SDK	0.916	0.016	0.016	0.052	27

Table 2.5: Hierarchical analysis of molecular variance of mtDNA haplotype frequencies for populations grouped to test putative source refugia for Common Eider populations breeding in North America and Scandinavia. Significant comparisons are in bold text ($P < 0.01$).

Regions[a]	No. Groups	Φ_{CT}	Φ_{SC}	Φ_{ST}
AC, BD, E, FG	4	**0.259**	**0.367**	**0.531**
A, BCD, E, FG	4	**0.273**	**0.364**	**0.537**
A, BCD, EG, F	4	**0.284**	**0.356**	**0.540**
AB, CDE, FG	3	**0.179**	**0.422**	**0.519**
A, BCDE, FG	3	**0.264**	**0.396**	**0.555**
A, BCD, EFG	3	**0.279**	**0.369**	**0.544**
A, BCDEG, F	3	**0.296**	**0.393**	**0.573**
A, BCDEFG	2	**0.325**	**0.417**	**0.606**
ABC, DEFG	2	**0.232**	**0.413**	**0.549**

[a]Regions; BOD and FLX (A), ALN and YKD (B), KTP (C), SHP, HDS, BCH, MSL, and BFN (D), NVS and NBW (E), SVD and SDK (F), and TRM (G)

Table 2.6: Results of demographic analyses for 12 microsatellite loci under the infinite allele model (IAM), stepwise mutation model (SMM), and two-phased model of mutation (TPM) and sequence data. Parameter estimates θ ($4N_e\mu$ for nuclear DNA, $2N_f\mu$ for mtDNA), exponential growth rate (g) with standard deviation (SD), and time of expansion (τ) calculated from mismatch distributions for each population. Significant comparisons are in bold text.

	ALN	YKD	BOD	FLX	KTP	BFN	HDS	SHP
Msats [a]								
IAM	Eq	**HExc**	**HExc**	**HExc**	Eq	Eq	Eq	Eq
SSM	**HDef**	**HDef**	**HDef**	**HDef**	**HDef**	**HDef**	**HDef**	**HDef**
TPM	Eq	Eq	Eq	Eq	Eq	Eq	Eq	**HDef**
Lamin A								
θ	**0.033**	**0.122**	**0.138**	**0.039**	**0.044**	**0.045**[b]	**0.008**	**0.019**
SD	0.003	0.007	0.012	0.005	0.010	0.022	0.001	0.002
g	**327.0**	**550.8**	**800.5**	**589.9**	**442.6**	**2339.5**	**672.9**	**400.5**
SD	61.9	31.3	46.2	88.5	102.2	355.3	198.7	64.4
Gapdh								
θ	**0.035**	**0.047**	**0.042**	**0.007**	**0.047**	0.004	**0.003**[b]	**0.011**
SD	0.003	0.003	0.004	0.001	0.009	0.002	0.001	0.001
g	**1212.9**	**400.0**	**875.8**	**307.2**[b]	**1778.2**	53.8	-140.3	**283.5**
SD	91.3	50.8	66.6	144.0	182.9	260.5	155.1	101.0
MtDNA								
θ	**0.012**	**0.023**	**0.007**	**0.007**	**0.021**	**0.017**	**0.050**	**0.034**
SD	0.001	0.002	0.001	0.001	0.003	0.005	0.014	0.006
g	**3673.2**	**534.1**	133.9	16.8	**303.4**	**1203.8**	**850.7**	**788.0**
SD	272.7	71.4	123.8	86.0	65.4	230.6	132.2	161.9
τ	0.992	5.709[c]	6.496	7.598	7.877[c]	2.758	3.555	3.863
95% CI	0.074, 1.363	1.559, 11.959	2.832, 10.496	2.950, 11.543	3.921, 15.290	0.443, 4.088	1.099, 7.133	1.082, 5.777

[a] Significant heterozygote deficiency (HDef) indicates population growth and heterozygote excess (Hexc) indicates a population decline, non-significant population estimates at equilibrium (Eq).

[b] Significant to $P < 0.05$, all others $P < 0.003$

[c] Population differs significantly from the sudden expansion model based on SSD statistic but not under Harpending's (1994) raggedness index

Table 2.6 cont.

	MSL	SVD	BCH	NBW	NVS	TRM	SDK
Msats [a]							
IAM	Eq	Eq	Eq	**HExc**	**HExc**	Eq	Eq
SSM	Eq	**HDef**	**HDef**	Eq	Eq	**HDef**	**HDef**
TPM	Eq	Eq	Eq	Eq	Eq	**HDef**	**HDef**
***Lamin* A**							
θ	0.010	**0.031**	**0.018**[b]	**0.530**	**0.100**	**0.025**	**0.009**
SD	0.008	0.005	0.008	0.052	0.010	0.003	0.002
g	373.3	**428.8**	352.3	**1130.7**	**562.2**	**464.0**	437.9
SD	287.9	84.4	272.0	34.8	38.8	63.8	208.5
Gapdh							
θ	100.0	**0.007**	**0.009**	**0.009**	**0.015**	**0.003**[b]	**0.003**[b]
SD	157.0	0.002	0.002	0.001	0.003	0.001	0.001
g	**4269.1**	242.9	**770.3**	**749.9**	**842.3**	-69.4	-127.1
SD	0.1	178.0	208.7	161.1	178.6	171.4	156.8
MtDNA							
θ	8.3	**0.010**	**0.006**[b]	**0.006**	**0.004**	**0.016**	0.008
SD	3.6	0.002	0.002	0.001	0.001	0.005	0.005
g	**6507.1**	260.9	254.9	132.9	102.1	**518.0**[b]	**10000**
SD	298.4	137.3	257.2	120.0	247.6	174.2	2514.1
τ	2.346	2.556	4.115	1.103[c]	3.000	2.689	0.497
95% CI	0.000,	1.181,	0.897,	0.429,	0.566,	0.682,	0.000,
	4.888	4.111	11.396	1.697	3.984	8.814	1.091

Table 2.7: Inferred demographic events of the nested clade analysis (only clades with significant D_c/D_n values are shown; Templeton 1998).

Inferred demographic event	Geographic units involved	Clade	Chain of inference
Continuous range expansion	ALN/KTP to FLX	I-2	1-2-11-12-NO
	TRM to BFN and NVS	I-12	1-19-20-2-11-12-NO
Past fragmentation and/or long distance colonization	BFN/BCH/HDS/MSL/SHP to BOD/FLX/YKD and NBW	I-4	1-2-3-5-15-NO
	BOD/FLX/HDS/KTP/SHP/ TRM/YKD to SVD	II-5	1-19-20-2-3-5-15-NO
	All regions	Total	1-2-3-5-15-NO
Restricted gene flow with isolation by distance	Among BFN, BOD, FLX, HDS, KTP, NBW, NVS, SHP, SVD, TRM, and YKD	I-10	1-2-3-4-NO
	Among BCH, BFN, HDS, SDK, SHP, SVD, and TRM	I-15	1-2-3-4-NO
	Among ALN, BOD FLX, KTP, and YKD	II-1	1-2-3-4-NO
	Among ALN, BCH, BFN, BOD, FLX, KTP, HDS, MSL, NBW, SHP, SVD, TRM, and YKD	II-2	1-2-11-17-4-NO
Restricted gene flow with some long distance colonization	BOD/FLX to KTP/HDS/SHP and TRM and YKD	I-21	1-2-3-5-6-7-8-YES
	BFN/BOD/FLX/HDS/KTP/ NBW/NVS/SHP/SVD/TRM/ YKD to BCH	II-3	1-2-3-5-6-7-YES
	BCH/BFN/HDS/SDK/SHP/ SVD/TRM to KTP/NVS/NBW	II-4	1-2-3-5-6-7-YES

Table 2.8: Migration matrix calculated from 12 microsatellite loci, nuclear introns *lamin* A and *gapdh*, and mtDNA control region. Receiving populations and θ ($N_e\mu$ or $N_f\mu$) are in bold text and population pairs with overlapping 95% confidence intervals are shaded in gray.

| Population Comparisons [a] | Number of Migrants per Generation ($N_e m$ or $N_f m$) | | |
	Microsatellites	Introns	MtDNA
Refugia			
North Slope	**0.8615**	**0.0036**	**0.0109**
	(0.8165–0.9088)	**(0.0032–0.0041)**	**(0.0080–0.0154)**
—Belcher	13.22	2.18	0.97
	(11.87–14.70)	(1.29–3.54)	(0.62–3.65)
—New Brunswick	6.91	0.46	1.94
	(6.07–7.86)	(0.16–1.07)	(0.55–5.68)
—Svalbard	8.29	2.41	0.00
	(7.34–9.35)	(1.46–3.86)	(0.00–0.93)
Belcher Is.	**0.8495**	**0.0070**	**0.0004**
	(0.7887–0.9168)	**(0.0061–0.0082)**	**(0.0003–0.0006)**
—North Slope	15.22	1.23	0.14
	(13.35–17.35)	(0.58–2.35)	(0.08–0.77)
—New Brunswick	13.44	1.62	0.55
	(11.76–15.38)	(0.84–2.93)	(0.15–1.74)
—Svalbard	14.96	0.53	0.28
	(13.11–17.07)	(0.17–1.29)	(0.04–1.12)
New Brunswick	**0.8556**	**0.0107**	**0.0007**
	(0.8093–0.9053)	**(0.0087–0.0134)**	**(0.0006–0.0009)**
—North Slope	8.26	6.10	0.00
	(7.28–9.37)	(3.14–11.34)	(0.00–0.15)
—Belcher	12.52	25.25	0.09
	(11.19–14.01)	(16.63–38.63)	(0.01–0.40)
—Svalbard	11.21	34.95	0.00
	(9.98–12.59)	(23.65–51.91)	(0.00–0.15)
Svalbard	**0.2165**	**0.0004**	**0.0040**
	(0.2059–0.2278)	**(0.0003–0.0004)**	**(0.0028–0.0060)**
—North Slope	4.53	2.03	0.00
	(3.99–5.15)	(1.27–3.19)	(0.00–0.81)
—Belcher	6.18	0.27	0.40
	(5.52–6.92)	(0.09–0.66)	(0.03–2.18)
—New Brunswick	7.05	5.54	3.95
	(6.30–7.87)	(3.93–7.80)	(1.55–9.65)

Table 2.8 cont.

Population Comparisons [a]	Number of Migrants per Generation (N_em or N_fm)		
	Microsatellites	Introns	MtDNA
S. m. v–nigrum			
Aleutians	**0.9373**	**0.0008**	**0.0003**
	(0.8759–1.0033)	**(0.0007–0.0020)**	**(0.0002–0.0004)**
—YK Delta	17.82	0.44	0.00
	(15.74–20.13)	(0.26–1.60)	(0.00–0.14)
—North Slope	16.21	2.39	0.15
	(14.30–18.35)	(1.81–7.14)	(0.10–0.56)
—Kent Pen.	17.92	0.41	0.00
	(15.86–20.23)	(0.24–1.52)	(0.00–0.14)
YK Delta	**0.5445**	**0.0000**	**0.0021**
	(0.5199–0.5708)	**(0.0000–0.0000)**	**(0.0016–0.0029)**
—Aleutians	11.14	0.01	0.00
	(10.09–12.29)	(0.00–0.05)	(0.00–0.31)
—North Slope	13.83	0.10	1.23
	(12.59–15.20)	(0.05–0.21)	(0.46–2.99)
—Kent Pen.	10.91	1.38	0.52
	(9.87–12.05)	(1.00–1.94)	(0.13–1.61)
North Slope	**0.5984**	**0.0050**	**0.0052**
	(0.5676–0.6314)	**(0.0045–0.0056)**	**(0.0040–0.0072)**
—Aleutians	10.79	5.97	0.62
	(9.63–12.09)	(4.46–7.93)	(0.15–1.95)
— YK Delta	18.28	1.03	1.25
	(16.55–20.19)	(0.58–1.73)	(0.44–3.16)
—Kent Pen.	25.50	1.03	0.21
	(23.26–27.96)	(0.58–1.74)	(0.14–1.04)
Kent Pen.	**0.6823**	**0.0061**	**0.0034**
	(0.6487–0.7171)	**(0.0045–0.0096)**	**(0.0021–0.0057)**
—Aleutians	11.66	85.90	0.53
	(10.48–12.95)	(53.19–159.22)	(0.29–3.26)
—YK Delta	15.43	43.39	3.17
	(13.97–17.01)	(24.97–85.69)	(0.95–9.84)
—North Slope	21.34	75.32	2.74
	(19.47–23.36)	(46.07–141.19)	(0.75–9.04)

Table 2.8 cont.

Population Comparisons [a]	Number of Migrants per Generation (N_em or N_fm)		
	Microsatellites	Introns	MtDNA
Central Canada and Svalbard			
Kent Pen.	**0.9449**	**0.0089**	**0.0024**
	(0.8953–0.9990)	**(0.0079–0.0102)**	**(0.0016–0.0037)**
—Baffin	15.88	0.15	0.90
	(14.24–17.73)	(0.01–0.63)	(0.20–3.18)
—Hudson Straits	13.03	2.99	0.60
	(11.62–14.62)	(1.78–4.84)	(0.10–2.47)
—Southampton	11.03	0.79	0.00
	(9.79–12.44)	(0.30–1.74)	(0.00–0.63)
—Svalbard	14.79	0.61	0.60
	(13.24–16.53)	(0.21–1.43)	(0.10–2.47)
—Belcher	13.53	0.15	0.60
	(12.08–15.16)	(0.01–0.63)	(0.10–2.47)
Baffin Is.	**0.9198**	**0.0020**	**0.0007**
	(0.8425–1.0053)	**(0.0016–0.0026)**	**(0.0004–0.0017)**
—Kent Pen.	21.50	0.00	0.00
	(18.59–24.92)	(0.00–0.32)	(0.00–2.43)
—Hudson Straits	30.15	5.14	0.78
	(26.28–34.68)	(2.93–8.89)	(0.04–6.56)
—Southampton	17.29	4.93	1.56
	(14.85–20.18)	(2.79–8.56)	(0.19–9.53)
—Svalbard	31.81	5.14	0.78
	(27.76–36.56)	(2.93–8.87)	(0.04–6.56)
—Belcher	23.20	2.38	11.66
	(20.09–26.85)	(1.15–4.68)	(3.83–40.08)
Hudson Straits	**0.5752**	**0.0008**	**0.0076**
	(0.5364–0.6181)	**(0.0007–0.0009)**	**(0.0062–0.0096)**
—Kent Pen.	11.31	0.80	0.34
	(9.88–12.95)	(0.36–1.60)	(0.07–1.13)
—Baffin	20.52	0.10	0.68
	(18.24–23.12)	(0.01–0.43)	(0.21–1.76)
—Southampton	9.23	4.25	0.51
	(7.97–10.72)	(2.80–6.36)	(0.36–1.46)
—Svalbard	23.00	6.48	0.68
	(20.50–25.84)	(4.50–9.27)	(0.21–1.76)
—Belcher	21.25	1.37	0.68
	(18.90–23.92)	(0.71–2.44)	(0.21–1.76)

Table 2.8 cont.

Population Comparisons [a]	Number of Migrants per Generation ($N_e m$ or $N_f m$)		
	Microsatellites	Introns	MtDNA
Southampton	**0.2855**	**0.0050**	**0.0100**
	(0.2688–0.3035)	**(0.0038–0.0068)**	**(0.0071–0.0147)**
—Kent Pen.	5.47	49.15	1.63
	(4.79–6.25)	(30.51–80.51)	(0.38–5.45)
—Baffin	8.50	22.04	0.00
	(7.54–9.57)	(12.33–39.44)	(0.00–1.08)
—Hudson Straits	5.92	55.88	25.05
	(5.17–6.78)	(35.13–90.50)	(13.84–46.43)
—Svalbard	10.99	0.00	4.36
	(9.92–12.31)	(0.00–1.22)	(1.63–10.86)
—Belcher	6.79	2.00	0.54
	(5.99–7.70)	(0.49–6.17)	(0.04–2.91)
Svalbard	**0.3228**	**0.0105**	**0.0125**
	(0.3062–0.3402)	**(0.0092–0.0120)**	**(0.0090–0.0180)**
—Kent Pen.	8.75	1.37	0.00
	(7.84–9.76)	(0.41–3.73)	(0.00–1.08)
—Baffin	13.21	14.77	0.55
	(11.97–14.55)	(8.81–24.84)	(0.04–2.91)
—Hudson Straits	10.13	2.34	2.22
	(9.11–11.25)	(0.88–5.50)	(0.62–6.58)
—Southampton	10.65	2.74	2.22
	(9.60–11.80)	(1.11–6.15)	(0.62–6.58)
—Belcher	8.55	4.12	6.09
	(7.66–9.52)	(1.91–8.46)	(2.56–13.87)
Belcher Is.	**0.6792**	**0.0035**	**0.0056**
	(0.6350–0.7275)	**(0.0027–0.0046)**	**(0.0032–0.0112)**
—Kent Pen.	14.10	1.18	0.00
	(12.43–15.99)	(0.52–2.37)	(0.00–2.80)
—Baffin	17.53	2.35	2.07
	(15.56–19.76)	(1.28–4.06)	(0.28–10.97)
—Hudson Straits	21.39	3.85	1.03
	(19.08–24.00)	(2.35–6.10)	(0.06–7.55)
—Southampton	10.89	1.88	41.37
	(9.53–12.45)	(0.96–3.41)	(17.95–106.19)
—Svalbard	13.03	1.04	1.03
	(11.46–14.81)	(0.43–2.18)	(0.06–7.55)

Table 2.8 cont.

Population Comparisons [a]	Number of Migrants per Generation ($N_e m$ or $N_f m$)		
	Microsatellites	Introns	MtDNA
Southern Canadian Populations			
Belcher Is.	**0.9651**	**0.0017**	**0.0194**
	(0.8899–1.0385)	**(0.0015–0.0020)**	**(0.0012–0.0346)**
—New Brunswick	8.78	3.27	8.93
	(7.53–10.14)	(2.06–5.09)	(3.07–25.25)
—Nova Scotia	13.13	4.65	4.09
	(11.41–14.97)	(3.09–6.94)	(1.05–14.07)
New Brunswick	**0.4708**	**0.0013**	**0.0015**
	(0.4449–0.4989)	**(0.0011–0.0016)**	**(0.0012–0.0020)**
—Belcher	7.66	13.56	0.41
	(6.74–8.72)	(9.06–20.26)	(0.29–1.11)
—Nova Scotia	19.26	21.35	0.21
	(17.40–21.33)	(14.93–30.63)	(0.04–0.71)
Nova Scotia	**0.4161**	**0.0102**	**0.0003**
	(0.3948–0.4390)	**(0.0088–0.0119)**	**(0.0002–0.0004)**
—Belcher	10.33	8.21	0.40
	(9.26–11.54)	(5.47–12.14)	(0.07–9.73)
—New Brunswick	15.95	13.80	1.79
	(14.45–17.62)	(9.78–19.37)	(1.12–13.24)
Scandinavia			
Svalbard	**0.3761**	**0.0041**	**0.0067**
	(0.3542–0.4002)	**(0.0034–0.0050)**	**(0.0041–0.0474)**
—Tromsø	16.76	9.62	12.96
	(15.03–18.68)	(6.11–14.98)	(5.23–133.55)
—Soderskar	11.47	9.38	11.44
	(10.13–12.95)	(5.94–14.66)	(4.48–120.53)
Tromsø	**1.0265**	**0.0022**	**0.0079**
	(0.9599–1.0990)	**(0.0019–0.0026)**	**(0.0059–0.0309)**
—Svalbard	24.08	3.88	3.68
	(21.49–27.00)	(2.39–6.14)	(1.67–21.92)
—Soderskar	16.14	10.26	0.56
	(14.22–18.28)	(7.22–14.53)	(0.37–24.49)
Soderskar	**0.4809**	**0.0103**	**0.0004**
	(0.4511–0.5116)	**(0.0086–0.0125)**	**(0.0000–0.0006)**
—Svalbard	11.12	3.31	0.07
	(9.81–12.75)	(1.77–5.91)	(0.01–0.26)
—Tromsø	9.20	15.31	0.00
	(8.09–10.42)	(10.44–22.47)	(0.00–0.00)

[a] Ninety-five percent confidence intervals are in parentheses.

Appendix 2.A: Localities of Common Eiders sampled* in this study.

Somateria mollissima v-nigrum

USA: Alaska, Aleutian Islands, Attu Island   52.938°N, 173.238°E
DAR157, MRP294, MRP295, UAMX1708

USA: Alaska, Aleutian Islands, Agattu Island   52.435°N, 173.576°E
MRP296, MRP297, MRP298, MRP299, MRP306, MRP307, MRP308, MRP309,
MRP310, MRP311, MRP312

USA: Alaska, Aleutian Islands, Alaid Island   52.763°N, 173.898°E
DBI2, DBI3, DBI4, DBI5, MRP285, MRP286, MRP287, MRP288, MRP289, MRP290,
MRP291, MRP292, MRP293, MRP300, MRP301, MRP302, MRP303, MRP304,
MRP305, MRP313, MRP314, MRP315, MRP316, MRP317, MRP318

USA: Alaska, Aleutian Islands, Amchitka Island   51.567°N, 178.878°E
MRP283, MRP284, MRP320, MRP321, MRP322, MRP323, MRP324, MRP325,
MRP326

USA: Alaska, Aleutian Islands, Adak Island 51.880°N, 176.658°W
PBAI935

Canada: Nunavut, Kent Peninsula 68.5°N, 107.0°W
COEI-M, DEAD-02, DEAD-03, DEAD-F, EUTH-M, KP1502, KP1505, KP1508,
KP1510, KP1512, KP1516, KP1517, KP1518, KP1519, KP1828, KP1829, KP1833,
KP1835, KP1836, KP1840, KP4553, KP4596, KP4597, KP4617, KP9816, KP9818,
KP9820, KP9823, KP9824, KP9825, KP9827, KP9828, KP9829, KP9830, KP9831,
KP9832, KP9833, KP9835, KP9836, KP9837, KP9838

Somateria mollissima borealis

Canada: Nunavut, Southampton Island   64.33°N, 84.667°W
H317, H321, H322, H325, H326, H327, H328, H329, H330, H333, H334, H335, H338,
H352, H25052, H25064, H25067, H25069, H25071, H25094, H25095, H25097,
H25269, H25276, H91488, H91574, H91575, H91579, H91697, H91698, H91701,
H91718, H91723, H91725, H91726, H91727, H91729, H91730, H91736, H91754,
H91756, H91981, H95196, H95967, H95969, H95970, H95972, H95974, H95975,
H95976, H95987, H95995

Canada: Nunavut, Baffin Island
M801, M803, M804, M805, M806, M808, M809, M810, M811, M812, M813, M814,
M815, M816, M817

Canada: Nunavut, Mansel Island 63.417°N, 77.917°W
F45, F47, F49

Canada: Nunavut, Baffin Island, Hudson Straits, Foxe Peninsula 64.1°N, 73.5°W
G33, G34, G37, G38, G39, G41, G42, G43, G49, G50, G51, G56, G57, G59, G60, G61,
G66, G68, G72, G73, G74, G75, G76, G77, G79, G80, G82, G85

Norway: Svalbard 78.2°N, 15.5°E
D1, D2, D3, D4, D5, D6, D7, D8, D9, D10, D11, D12, D13, D14, D15, D16, D17, D18,
D19, D20, D21, D22, D23, D24, D25, D26, D27, D28, D29, D30, D31, D32, D33, D34,
D35, D36, D37

Somateria mollissima sedentaria

Canada: Nunavut, Belcher Islands 56.183°N, 79.250°W
T11, T12, T13, T14, T15, T16, T17, T18, T19, T20, TB01, TB02, TB03, TB04, TF01,
TF02, TF03, TF04, TM01, TM02, TM03, TM04

Somateria mollissima dresseri

Canada: New Brunswick 45.5°N, 67.0°W
BD#, BNB, B6, B33, B43, B44, B45, B47, B48, B49, B51, B52, B53, B99, B209, B244,
B515, B609, B5170, B21627, B25423, B26170, B40194, B40622, B45320, B45509,
B48222, B49008, B49028, B49055, B49071, B49073, B49583, B59510, B59513,
B59516, B59519, B59521, B59524, B85408

Canada: Nova Scotia 44.716°N, 65.200°W
C1, C10, C14, C15, C17, C20, C21, C24, C30, C32, C34, C37, C39, C42, C45, C46,
C50, C52, C53, C54, C55, C56, C57, C60, C61, C62, C63, C64, C66, C67, C68, C69,
C70, C71, C73, C77, C80, C81, C83, C116

Somateria mollissima mollissima

Norway: Troms, Tromsø 69.7°N, 18.9°E
E9, E10, E13, E15, E18, E20, E25, E28, E33, E35, E75, E86, E95, E98, E104, E107,
E107-2, E117, E118, E123, E129, E137, E138, E139, E142, E148, E150, E153, E154,
E162, E167, E175, E188, E191, E192, E195, E200, E202

Finland: Southern Finland, Soderskar 60.25°N, 25.5°E
A510178, A510588, A510658, A510678, A580197, A580297, A580397, A580497,
A584297, A584393, A586797, A586897, A588097, A588597, DT12063, DT35166,
DX1028, DX2714, DX3241, DX4333, DX4739, DX5559, DX7428, DX35013,
DX120319, DX12218, DX324119

**Sample IDs starting with UAM are located at the University of Alaska Museum, Fairbanks, Alaska. Remaining samples are located in non-museum research collections.

Appendix 2.B: Variable positions and frequency (*n*) of nuclear intron *lamin* A alleles reconstructed in PHASE in Common Eiders.

	7112599111111111111222 899508011566677779277 467507814595023	*n*
Allele01	GGACCCCCTGTACGCCGCCTGA	23
Allele02	GGACCCCCTGTACGTCGCCTGA	1
Allele03	GGACCCCCCGTACGCCGCCTGA	76
Allele04	GGACCCCCCGTACGCCGCCTAG	2
Allele05	GGACCCCCCGTACGCCGCCCGA	1
Allele06	GGACCCCCCGTACGCCGCTTGA	4
Allele07	GGACCCCCCGTACGCCACCTGA	6
Allele08	GGACCCCCCGTACGTCGTCTGA	5
Allele09	GGACCCCCCGTCCGCCGCCTGA	5
Allele10	GGACCCCCCGTCCGCCGCCCGA	2
Allele11	GGACCCCCCGTCCGCCGCTTGA	6
Allele12	GGACCCCCCGTCCGCCGCTTAG	1
Allele13	GGACCCCCCGTCCGCTGCCTGA	1
Allele14	GGACCCCCCGTCCGTCGTCTGA	1
Allele15	GGACCCCCCGTCCGTCGTCTAG	2
Allele16	GGACCCCCCGGACGCCGCCTGA	1
Allele17	GGACCCGCTGTACGCCGCCTGA	5
Allele18	GGACCCGCTGTACGCCGCCCGA	2
Allele19	GGACCCGCTGTCCGCCGCCTGA	9
Allele20	GGACCCGCCGTACGCCGCCTGA	30
Allele21	GGACCCGCCGTACGCCGCCCGA	1
Allele22	GGACCCGCCGTACGCCACCTGA	2
Allele23	GGACCCGCCGTACGTCGCCTGA	3
Allele24	GGACCCGCCGTCCGCCGCCTGA	207
Allele25	GGACCCGCCGTCCGCCGCCTAG	4
Allele26	GGACCCGCCGTCCGCCGCCCGA	177
Allele27	GGACCCGCCGTCCGCCGCCCAG	1
Allele28	GGACCCGCCGTCCGCCGCTTGA	29
Allele29	GGACCCGCCGTCCGCCGTCTGA	24
Allele30	GGACCCGCCGTCCGCCACCTGA	2
Allele31	GGACCCGCCGTCCGCTGCCTGA	4
Allele32	GGACCCGCCGTCCGCTGTCTGA	128
Allele33	GGACCCGCCGTCCGCTGTCTAG	5
Allele34	GGACCCGCCGTCCGTCGCCTGA	37
Allele35	GGACCCGCCGTCCGTCGCCTAG	1
Allele36	GGACCCGCCGTCCGTCGCCCGA	3
Allele37	GGACCCGCCGTCCGTCGTCTGA	195
Allele38	GGACCCGCCGTCCGTCGTCTAG	6
Allele39	GGACCCGCCGTCCGTCGTCCGA	1
Allele40	GGACCCGCCGTCCGTCGTCCAG	1

Appendix 2.B cont.

	7112599111111111111222 899508011566677779277 467507814595023	*n*
Allele41	GGACCCGCCGTCCGTTGTCTGA	3
Allele42	GGACCCGCCGTCCACTGCCTGA	1
Allele43	GGACCCGCCGTCCACTGTCTGA	10
Allele44	GGACCCGCCGTCTGCCGCCCGA	1
Allele45	GGACCCGCCATCCGCCGCCTGA	11
Allele46	GGACCCGTCGTCCGCCGCCTGA	1
Allele47	GGACCCGTCGTCCGCCGCCCGA	4
Allele48	GGACCCGTCGTCCGCCGCTTGA	1
Allele49	GGACCGGCCGTACGCCGCCTGA	3
Allele50	GGACCGGCCGTCCGCCGCCTGA	11
Allele51	GGACCGGCCGTCCGCCGCCCGA	5
Allele52	GGACCGGCCGTCCGCTGTCTGA	3
Allele53	GGACCGGCCGTCCGTCGCCTGA	10
Allele54	GGACCGGCCGTCCGTCGTCTGA	3
Allele55	GGACCGGCCATCCGCCGCCTGA	1
Allele56	GGACTCCCCGTCCGCCGCCTGA	2
Allele57	GGACTCGCTGTCCGCCGCCTGA	3
Allele58	GGACTCGCCGTCCGCCGCCTGA	41
Allele59	GGACTCGCCGTCCGCCGCCCGA	1
Allele60	GGACTCGCCGTCCGCCGCTTGA	19
Allele61	GGATCCCCCGTACGCCGCCTGA	1
Allele62	GGATCCGCCGTCCGCCGCCTGA	1
Allele63	GAGCCCGCCGTCCGCCGCCCGA	1
Allele64	GAGCCCGCCGTCCGCTGTCTGA	1
Allele65	GAGCCCGCCATCCGCCGCCTGA	2
Allele66	CGACCCCCCGTACGCCGCCTGA	1
Allele67	CGACCCGCCGTCCGCCGCCTGA	13
Allele68	CGACCCGCCGTCCGCCGCCTAG	1
Allele69	CGACCCGCCGTCCGCCGCCCGA	6
Allele70	CGACCCGCCGTCCGTCGTCTGA	3

Appendix 2.C: Variable positions and frequency (*n*) of nuclear intron *gapdh* alleles reconstructed in PHASE in Common Eiders.

	124448111111111222233 623893122344 6789355756 4296565062228768	*n*
Allele01	CCCCGGCCAGCGAAGGCGAGAG	5
Allele02	CCCCGGCCAGCGAAGGCGAGGG	1
Allele03	CCCCGGCCAGCGAAGGCGGGAG	86
Allele04	CCCCGGCCAGCGAACACGGGAG	9
Allele05	CCCCGGCCAGCGGAGGCGAGAG	134
Allele06	CCCCGGCCAGCGGAGGCGGGAG	11
Allele07	CCCCGGCCAGCGGAGGTGAGAG	1
Allele08	CCCCGGCCAGCGGAGGTGGGAG	1
Allele09	CCCCGGCCAGCGGGGGCGAGAG	10
Allele10	CCCCGGCCAGCGGGGGTGAGAG	4
Allele11	CCCCGGCCAGTGAAGGCGAGAG	5
Allele12	CCCCGGCCAGTGAAGGCGGGAG	18
Allele13	CCCCGGCCAGTGAAGGCGGAAG	1
Allele14	CCCCGGCCAACGAAGGCGGGAG	1
Allele15	CCCCGGCCAACGGAGGCGAGAG	2
Allele16	CCCCGGCCAACGGAGGCGGGAG	5
Allele17	CCCCGGCCAACGGAGGCGGGAA	1
Allele18	CCCCGGCCAACGGGGGCGAGAG	82
Allele19	CCCCGGCCAACGGGGGCGGGAG	10
Allele20	CCCCGGCCAACGGGGGCGGAAG	1
Allele21	CCCCGGCCAACGGGGGCAAGAG	1
Allele22	CCCCGGCCGGCGAAGGCGAGAG	1
Allele23	CCCCGGCCGGCGGAGGCGAGAG	258
Allele24	CCCCGGCCGGCGGAGGCGGGAG	73
Allele25	CCCCGGCCGGCGGAGGCGGAAG	5
Allele26	CCCCGGCCGGCGGAGGTGAGAG	3
Allele27	CCCCGGCCGGCGGGGGCGGGAG	15
Allele28	CCCCGGCCGGCGGGGGCGGAAG	1
Allele29	CCCCGGCCGGCAGAGGCGAGAG	2
Allele30	CCCCGGCTAGCGGAGGCGAGAG	3
Allele31	CCCCGGCTAGCGGAGGTGAGAG	132
Allele32	CCCCGGCTAGCGGAGGTGAGGG	7
Allele33	CCCCGGCTAGCGGAGGTGGGAG	3
Allele34	CCCCGGCTAGCGGGGGTGAGAG	1
Allele35	CCCCGGGCAGCGGAGGCGAGAG	1
Allele36	CCCCGACTAGCGGAGGTGAGAG	1
Allele37	CCCCAGCCAGCGAACACGAGAG	5
Allele38	CCCCAGCCAGCGAACACGGGAG	18
Allele39	CCCTGGCCAGCGGAGGTGAGAG	1
Allele40	CCCTGGCCGGCGGAGGCGAGAG	3

Appendix 2.C cont.

	124448111111111222233 62389312234467893557 56 4296565062228768	*n*
Allele41	CCTCGGCCAGCGGGGGTGAGAG	1
Allele42	CCTCGGCTAGCGGAGGTGAGAG	2
Allele43	CTCCGGCCAGCGGAGGCGAGAG	3
Allele44	ACCCGGCCAGCGAAGGCGGGAG	1
Allele45	ACCCGGCCAGCGGAGGCGAGAG	8
Allele46	ACCCGGCCAACGGGGGCGAGAG	2
Allele47	ACCCGGCCGGCGGAGGCGAGAG	6
Allele48	ACCCGGCCGGCGGAGGCGGGAG	1

Appendix 2.D: Variable positions and frequency (*n*) for each mtDNA control region haplotype from Common Eiders (dots indicate missing data; – indicates deletion).

	3411223334456666777788111111133344555 1212156248578914590601116724768555 31562445385589	*n*
Hap01	. . . . AACGCGGTCCCACCTAGTGCATCTTTCCGTCT	57
Hap02	. . . . AACGCGGTCCCACCTAGTGCATCTTTCCGTTT	2
Hap03	. . . . AACGCGGTCCCATCTAGTGCATCTTTCCGTCT	17
Hap04	. . . . GACGCGATCCCACCCAGAGCATCTTTTCGTTT	109
Hap05	. . . . GACGCGATCCCACCCAGAGCGTCTTTCCGTTT	14
Hap06	. . . . GACGCGGTCCCACCCAGAGCATCTTTCCGTTT	7
Hap07	. . . . GACGCGGTCCCGCCCAGAGCATCTTTCCGTCT	12
Hap08	. . . . GACGCGGTCCCGCCCGGAACATTTTTCCGTCT	3
Hap09	. . . . GACGCGGTCCCGCCCGGAACATTTTTCTGTCT	1
Hap10	. . . . GACGCGGTCCCGCCCGGAGCATCCTTCCGTCT	3
Hap11	GTTTGACGCGGTCCCGCCCGGAGCATCTTTCCGTCT	27
Hap12	. . . . AACACGGTCCCACCTAGTGCATCTTTCCGTCT	2
Hap13	. . . . GACGCGGTCCCACCCAGAGCATCCTTCCGTCT	11
Hap14	. . . . GACGCGGTCCCACCTAGAGCAGCTTTCCGTCT	1
Hap15	. . . . GACGCGGTCCCGCCCGAAGCATCTTTCCGTCT	1
Hap16	. . . . GGCGCGATCCCACCCAGAGCATCTTTTCGTTT	5
Hap17	GTTTGACGCGGTCCCGCCCGGAGCATTTTTCCGTCT	12
Hap18	GTTTGACGCGGTCCTACCCGGAGCATTTTTCCGTCT	2
Hap19	GTTTGACGCGGTCCTGCCCGGAGCATTTTTCCGTCT	25
Hap20	. . . . AACGCAGTCCCACCTAGTGCATCTTTCCGTCT	10
Hap21	. . . . GACGCGATCCCACCCAGAGCATCCTTTCGTTT	5
Hap22	. . . . GACGCGATTCCACCCAGAGCGTCTTTCCGTTT	5
Hap23	. . . . AACGCGATTCCACCCAGAGCGTCTTTCCGTTT	1
Hap24	. . . . GGCGCGATCCCACCCAGAGCATCCTTTCGTTT	1
Hap25	ACTTGACGTGATCCCACCCAGAGCGTCTTTCCGTTT	21
Hap26	ATTTGACGTGATCCCACCCAGAGCGTCTTTCCGTTT	2
Hap27	ACTTGACGTGATCCCACCCAGAGTGTCTTTCCGTTT	1
Hap28	ACTTGACGTGATCCCACCCAGAGCATCTTTCCGTTT	1
Hap29	ACTTGACGCGATCCCACCCAGAGTATCTTTTCGTTT	10
Hap30	. . . . GACGCGATCCCACCCAGAGCATCTTTTCATTT	5
Hap31	. . . . GACGCAGTCCCACCCAGAGCATCTTTCCGTCT	3
Hap32	. . . . GACGTGATCCCACCCAGAGTATCTTTTCGTTT	1
Hap33	ATTTGACACGATCCCACCCAGAGCATCTTTTCGTTC	1
Hap34	ACTTAACGCGATCCCACCCAGAGCGTCTTTCCGTTT	1
Hap35	. . . . GACGCGATCCCACCCAGAGCATCTTTCCGTTT	5
Hap36	ACTTGATGCGATCCCACCCAGAGCATCTTTCCGTTT	1
Hap37	. . . . AACACGGTCCCACCTAGTGCATCCTTCCATCT	2
Hap38	. . . . GACGCGGTCCCACCCAGAGCATCTTTTCGTTT	3
Hap39	. . . . AACGCGGTCCCACCTAGTGCATTTTTCCGTCT	1
Hap40	. . . . GACACGATCCCACCCAGAGCATCTTTCCGTTT	2

Appendix 2.D cont.

	3411223334456666777788111111133344555 1212156248578914590601116724768555 31562445385589	*n*
Hap41	. . . .GACGCGATCCCACCCAGAGCATCTTTTCGTCT	1
Hap42	. . . .GACACGATCCCACCCAGAGCATCTTTTCGTTT	6
Hap43	ACTTGACGCGATCCCACCCAGAGCGTCTTCCCGGTT	1
Hap44	. . . .GACGCGATCCCACCCAGAGCGTCTTCCCGTTT	4
Hap45	. . . .AACGCGGTCCCACCCAGTGCATCTTTCGTCT	1
Hap46	. . . .GACGCGATCCCACCCAGAGCGTCTTTCCGTCT	1
Hap47	. . . .GACGCGATTCCACCCAGAGCATCTTTCCGTTT	2
Hap48	ACTTGACGCGGTCCCACCCAGAGCATTCTTCCGTCT	1
Hap49	ACTTGACGCGGTCCCACCCAGAGCATCTTTCCGTCT	26
Hap50	ACTTGACGCGGTTCCACCCAGAGCATCTTTCCGTCT	2
Hap51	GCCTGACGCGGTCCCACCCAGAGCATCTTTCCGTCT	1
Hap52	ACTTGACGCGATCCCACCTAGAGCATCTTTCCGTTT	1
Hap53	ACCTGACGCGGTCCCACCCAGAGCATCTTTCCGTCT	1
Hap54	ACTTGACGCGGTCCCACCCAGAGTATCTTTCCGTCT	1
Hap55	ACTTGACGCGACCCCACCCAGAGCGTCTTTCCGTTT	3
Hap56	ACTTGACGCGGTCACACTCAGAGCATCTTTCCGTCT	1
Hap57	ACTTGACGCGATCCCACCCAGAGCATCTTTCCATTC	2
Hap58	ACTTGACGCGATCCCACCCAGAGCATCTCTTCGTTT	1
Hap59	ACTTGACGCGATCCCACCCGGAGCATCTTTTCGTTT	1
Hap60	ACTCGACGCG-TCCCACCCAGAGCATCTTTCCGTTT	1
Hap61	ACTTGACACGATCCCACCCAGAGCATCCTTTCGTTT	1
Hap62	ACTTGACGCGATCCCACCCAGAGCATCTTCCCGTTT	1
Hap63	ACTTGACGCGGTCCCACCTAGAGCATCTTTCCGTCT	1
Hap64	ACTTGGCGCGATCCCACCCAGAGCATCTTCTCGTTT	2

80

PART 3: Do Waterfowl Nest in Kin Groups? Evidence from the Common Eider (*Somateria mollissima*) Breeding in the Beaufort Sea, Alaska

Abstract

We investigated local genetic associations among female Common Eiders nesting on two island groups in the Beaufort Sea, Alaska, in 2000–2003 using multivariate autocorrelation analyses and highly variable microsatellite markers. Global analyses revealed strong correlations between genetic and geographic distances among years and island groups (Pearson's r = 0.534 - 0.813, P < 0.001), and between genetic relatedness (r$_{xy}$) and geographic distance (Pearson's r = -0.012 to -0.181, P < 0.001), indicating that females are nesting in closer proximity to more genetically related individuals. Nonrandom genetic associations also were observed using a global spatial autocorrelation analyses for distance classes up to 1000 m in Simpson Lagoon but not Mikkelsen Bay. Nearest-neighbor analyses identified clusters of genetically related females in both Simpson Lagoon and Mikkelsen Bay. Differences in the degree of genetic structuring between island groups may be attributable to the availability or distribution of nesting habitat, as Simpson Lagoon has three islands with colonies, whereas Mikkelsen Bay has only one. Significant structuring observed at microgeographic scales indicates eiders may nest in kin groups. Though the underlying mechanism enabling female eiders discriminate kin is unknown, waterfowl may achieve kin recognition indirectly through association during brood rearing.

Introduction

Genetic consequences of philopatric behavior have been demonstrated in several taxa (e.g., Tiedemann et al. 1999, Scribner et al. 2001, Avise 2004). Dispersal homogenizes allelic frequencies, whereas natal and breeding philopatry can lead to patterns of spatial genetic subdivision among populations. Unfortunately, dispersal is difficult to study because it often requires long-term demographic studies (Koenig et al. 1996), and in species that are highly mobile, estimates may be more difficult to obtain since individuals may disperse out of the study site. Genetic studies frequently have been used to assess intergenerational dispersal (gene flow) among populations. However, most studies that have characterized population genetic structure have assessed allelic frequency differences within and among populations and are not designed to detect local groupings of genetically related individuals within populations, which would be expected in species that exhibit restricted dispersal (Double et al. 2005).

Researchers have hypothesized several mechanisms promoting philopatric behavior within species, including selective advantages of increased assistance from relatives during the breeding season (Lessells et al. 1994); decreased competition and aggression between related or familiar neighbors (Greenwood et al. 1979, Waldman 1988, Eason and Hannon 1994); or site familiarity (Anderson et al. 1992). Kin association and philopatry may have different effects on spatial genetic structure at the inter-individual scale. Individuals preferentially breeding near more genetically-related individuals might create clusters of non-random genetic associations among individuals at fine-spatial scales (Fowler et al. 2004, Double et al. 2005). Conversely, if individuals are philopatric to an area alone, fine-scale spatial associations may not be observed depending upon the size of the study area and density of the population.

Here we investigate microgeographic genetic structuring in Common Eiders (*Somateria mollissima*). Pacific Common Eiders (*S. m. v-nigrum*) breeding on coastal barrier islands in the Beaufort Sea, Alaska, nest in association with driftwood. Female Common Eiders either nest in dense colonies or scattered locations on islands because of the availability of nesting habitat (Goudie et al. 2000). As observed for other waterfowl, female Common Eiders exhibit high natal and breeding philopatry (Goudie et al. 2000), which promotes high levels of genetic partitioning among populations at mitochondrial DNA (mtDNA; Tiedemann et al. 1999, Tiedemann et al. 2004, Sonsthagen et al. submitted a, b). Furthermore, researchers investigating the colonial nesting of eiders breeding in Hudson Bay (*S. m. sedentaria*) hypothesized that eiders breeding in groups were composed of extended family, as some groups of Common Eiders exhibited greater nesting synchrony than expected by chance (Schmutz et al. 1983). Variance in egg shape among females within these groups suggested genetic relatedness. In addition, Common Eiders (*S. m. borealis*) breeding on Southampton Island in Hudson Bay arrive to the colony, nest, and brood rear in female kin-based social groups, which were determined using molecular techniques (McKinnon 2005).

We used a multivariate autocorrelation analyses developed by Double et al. (2005) to investigate local genetic associations among female Common Eiders breeding on 12 islands in the Beaufort Sea. Given evidence from previous studies in other subspecies of Common Eiders and high natal and breeding philopatry observed for female Common Eiders, we predicted that the Beaufort Sea eiders nest in close association with more genetically related individuals than expected by chance. We also hypothesized that, due to differences in nesting habitat, spatial genetic associations may not be as pronounced as those observed within Hudson Bay colonies. Seasonal arctic storms in the Beaufort Sea dramatically modify island topology, changing where nesting habitat is located annually (Noel et al. 2005). In contrast, Hudson Bay Common Eiders nest on coastal wetland tundra habitat (Goudie et al. 2000) that has remained relatively unchanged across consecutive breeding seasons.

Methods

Sample Collection

Blood or feather samples were collected from breeding female Common Eiders opportunistically during mark-recapture and monitoring efforts on barrier islands in the Beaufort Sea, Alaska, from 2000–2003. Samples were collected from two island groups, consisting of 12 islands in total. The western group, hereafter called Simpson Lagoon, consists of five islands: Stump (70.419°N 148.601°W), Wannabe (70.437°N 148.725°W), Egg (70.440°N 148.739°W), Long (70.480°N 148.937°W), and Spy (70.564°N 149.895°W) islands (Fig. 2.1A). The eastern group, hereafter called Mikkelsen Bay; consists of seven islands: Camp (70.172°N 146.226°W), Point Thomson (70.186°N 146.325°W), Mary Saches (70.200°N 146.207°W), North Star (70.225°N 146.347°W), Duchess (70.233°N 146.405°W), Alaska (70.233°N 146.559°W), and Challenge (70.237°N 146.640°W) islands (Fig. 2.1B). Distances between islands within each of the two island groups ranged from 1.2–49.2 km, and distances between islands located in Simpson and Mikkelsen Bay ranged from 78.1–143.1 km. Two islands, Camp and Wannabe, are not official names of islands on any recognized maps, but were given these names for the purpose of identifying areas in this study.

Females were captured on nests using a dip net during initial nest searching efforts, or with a bow net during late-incubation (Sayler 1962). Blood was collected from the tarsal, brachial, or jugular veins and placed in lysis buffer (Longmire et al. 1988). Feather samples were collected from nest bowls from unsampled females and stored in silica gel desiccant at room temperature. After returning from the field, samples were archived at −80°C at the U. S. Geological Survey Molecular Ecology Laboratory, Anchorage, Alaska. Genomic DNAs were extracted using either a "salting out" protocol described in Medrano et al. (1990) with modifications described in Sonsthagen et al. (2004), or a QIAGEN DNeasy Tissue Kit (QIAGEN, Valencia, CA). Concentrations of genomic DNA extracts were quantified using fluorometry and diluted to 50 ng/µL working solutions.

Microsatellite Genotyping

Primers used for microsatellite genotyping of Common Eiders (n = 317) were obtained via cross-species screening of microsatellite primers developed for other waterfowl. We screened 12 Common Eiders at 50 microsatellite loci reported to be variable for other waterfowl species and selected 14 microsatellite loci found to be polymorphic: Aph02, Aph08, Aph20, Aph23 (Maak et al. 2003); Bcaμl, Bcaμll, Hhiμ3 (Buchholz et al. 1998); Cm09 (Maak et al. 2000); Sfiμ10 (Libants et al. unpubl. data); Smo4, Smo7, Smo08, Smo10, and Smo12 (Paulus and Tiedemann 2003). Microsatellites were amplified using the polymerase chain reaction (PCR), and products were electrophoresed following protocols described in Sonsthagen et al. (2004) for tailed primers (Aph02, Aph08, Aph20, Aph23, Cm09, Smo4, Smo7, Smo08, Smo10, and Smo12) and Pearce et al. (2005) for direct-labeled primers (Bcaμl, Bcaμll, Hhiμ3, and Sfiμ10). For quality control purposes, 10% of the samples were randomly selected, re-amplified, and genotyped in duplicate.

Data Analysis

Allelic frequencies, and expected and observed heterozygosities for each microsatellite locus were calculated in GENEPOP 3.1 (Raymond and Rousset 1995) and FSTAT 2.9.3 (Goudet 1995, 2001). Hardy Weinberg Equilibrium and linkage disequilibrium were tested in GENEPOP using the default parameters (Markov chain parameters: dememorization number 1000, number of batches 100, and number of iterations per batch 10,000), adjusting for multiple comparisons using Bonferroni corrections ($\alpha = 0.05$). To determine if we could accurately identify individuals, and therefore assess levels of relatedness among individuals, probabilities of identity for a randomly mating population (PID) and among siblings (PIDsib) were calculated in Gimlet 1.3.3 (Valière 2002) using genotypes from the 14 microsatellite loci.

Queller and Goodnight's (1989) index of relatedness (rxy) was calculated overall and among pairs of individuals breeding on each island group within a given year using IDENTIX 1.1 (Belkhir et al. 2002). Relatedness values range from −1 to 1, where rxy equals 0.5 for full-sibling relationships, 0.25 for half-sibling relationships, and 0 for unrelated individuals. Genetic discordance among sampled areas may cause incorrect relatedness values, as values measure genetic differences in overall allelic frequency (Queller and Goodnight 1989). Therefore, spatial analyses of individuals were partitioned by island groups because Sonsthagen et al. (submitted a) observed significant genetic differentiation between Mikkelsen Bay and Simpson Lagoon. Squared genetic distance was calculated between pairs of individuals within each island group following the method of Smouse and Peakall (1999) in GenAlEx 6 (Peakall and Smouse 2006). Geographic distances among sampled nests were calculated using Universal Transverse Mercator (UTM) coordinates.

Overall correlation between genetic similarity and geographic distance at the population level was assessed using Mantel tests implemented in the software zt 1.0 (Bonnet and Van de Peer 2002). Significance of Pearson correlation coefficients were assessed using a randomization procedure, where the original value of the statistic was compared to the distribution of a random reallocation of the distance values in one of the matrices (randomization = 10,000).

Global spatial autocorrelation analyses were conducted in GenAlEx to further investigate spatial partitioning of individuals within an island group in a given year, as weak or scattered patterns may not be detected using a simple Mantel analysis. Genetic and geographic matrices calculated in GenAlEx were used to determine

Results

Multi-locus genotypes were obtained for 317 individuals. The number of alleles per locus for the 14 polymorphic microsatellite loci ranged from 3–44 (Table 3.1), with an average 11.3 alleles per locus. The average number of alleles per island group in a given year ranged from 6.21–8.79 (Table 3.2). The observed heterozygosity for each area in a given year ranged from 56.1–60.6% with an overall value of 57.7% (Table 3.2). All loci did not significantly deviate from Hardy-Weinberg equilibrium and were in linkage equilibrium ($P_{adj.} > 0.05$).

We calculated an overall PID of 3.2×10^{-12} for a population composed of randomly mating individuals and 5.3×10^{-5} for siblings using genotypes collected from 14 microsatellite loci (Table 3.1). These denominator values are much larger than the population breeding on the western Beaufort Sea (approximately 500 nests found on the islands each year; Johnson 2000), which gave us confidence in identifying individuals correctly among years. Overall r_{xy} values from Mikkelsen Bay and Simpson Lagoon ranged from -0.037 to -0.008, and -0.063 to -0.014, respectively (Table 3.2). Mean r_{xy} values close to zero indicate that, on average, Mikkelsen Bay and Simpson Lagoon are composed of unrelated females. Variances were large (Table 3.2), indicating populations are comprised of some highly related individuals, and some individuals that are not closely related.

Significant correlations between genetic distance and r_{xy} values with geographic distance were observed among years and island groups (Table 3.3), indicating that more genetically related individuals are nesting geographically closer to each other than expected by chance. Fine-scale spatial structure was observed in Simpson Lagoon at the 0–50 m distance class in 2001; 0–100, 0–250, 0–500, and 0–1000 m distance classes in 2002; and 0–10 and 0–25 m distance classes in 2003 (Fig. 3.2A). Nesting female Common Eiders in Mikkelsen Bay did not depart from a nonrandom distribution of genotypes at any distance class (Fig. 3.2B).

For Common Eiders nesting in Simpson Lagoon, 0–29% of the lr values calculated for the four nearest neighbors were positive (one-tailed P-values = 0.001–0.046; Table 3.4). Positive values clustered around Stump, Long, and Egg Islands (Fig. 3.3). Within Mikkelsen Bay, 0–14% of the lr values were positive (one-tailed P-values = 0.004–0.046; Table 3.4) for the four nearest neighbors. Positive lr values clustered around Camp, Duchess, Alaska, and Challenge Islands (Fig. 3.3). A similar number and distribution of positive values were observed among years and island groups for estimates based on four, six, eight, and ten nearest neighbors (data not shown).

Discussion

Global correlation analyses revealed fine-scale genetic structure among nesting females in the Beaufort Sea, indicating that genetically related individuals nested closer to each other than expected by chance. The pattern of spatial genetic structure revealed by global autocorrelation analyses using distance class sampling was not strong. Low r values were observed for Simpson Lagoon in 2002 and 2003, and females nesting in Mikkelsen Bay did not deviate from a random distribution. Differences in the degree of genetic structuring between Simpson Lagoon and Mikkelsen Bay may be attributable to the availability or distribution of nesting habitat. Three islands (Egg, Long, and Stump) contain Common Eider colonies within Simpson Lagoon; approximately 50, 35, and 155 nests were found in 2003 on each, respectively (J. Reed unpubl. data). In Mikkelsen Bay, only one island, Duchess, contains a colony, with approximately 90 nests found in 2003 (J. Reed unpubl. data). On islands without colonies, approximately 10–20 nests were found scattered across each. McKinnon (2005) found that females nesting in high densities had higher levels of relatedness among focal females and the two nearest females than those nesting in low-density areas. Females in high density nesting areas may prefer to nest in closer proximity to more genetically-related individuals because of reduced aggression among kin (Greenwood et al. 1979, Waldman 1988, Eason and Hannon 1994). In contrast, on low nesting density islands there may not be an advantage to nesting in close association with kin due to presumably fewer interactions among neighbors. Alternatively, females in Simpson Lagoon may simply be able to nest in closer proximity to kin because of the availability of suitable habitat.

Microgeographic genetic structure was uncovered by the two-dimensional local spatial autocorrelation analysis, indicating that females are nesting in association with more genetically related females. Clusters of non-random genetic associations were observed in Simpson Lagoon and in Mikkelsen Bay. Double et al. (2005) hypothesized that clusters of local positive genetic autocorrelation observed may exist because of an individual being more successful reproductively. In highly philopatric species, progeny from successful lineages might cluster around natal sites. Female Common Eiders have been reported to be philopatric to natal sites (Swennen 1990), areas within colonies (Cooch 1965), and to exhibit fidelity to specific nest bowls (Bustnes and Erikstad 1993). Therefore, clusters of related females may be due to extreme natal and breeding philopatry coupled with high reproductive output.

Kin recognition among female Common Eiders also may contribute to the local clusters of positive genetic autocorrelation observed. Kin-based clusters have been postulated to occur among nesting females on the Belcher Islands, Hudson Bay (Schmutz et al. 1983). Furthermore, female eiders breeding on Southampton Island, Hudson Bay, form kin-based social groups during colony arrival, nesting, and colony departure, which suggests some form of kin recognition (McKinnon 2005). A variety of mechanisms enabling individuals to discriminate kin have been identified (Komdeur and Hatchwell 1999) and could be achieved indirectly though association (Hatchwell et al. 2001, Komdeur et al. 2004). In the highly philopatric Barnacle Goose (*Branta leucopsis*), females preferentially nested in kin groups that were based on kin recognition rather than extreme natal philopatry, as females that bred away from natal sites nested in close geographic proximity to sisters that they were familiar with as brood mates (van der Jeugd et al. 2002). If recognition among female Common Eiders influences nest site selection, this may explain, in part, why only some females nest in kin groups. In Common Eiders, females may rear broods alone or randomly form brood amalgamations (i.e., not kin-based; Öst et al. 2005). Therefore, Common Eiders may nest in close proximity to brood mates, independent of their genetic relatedness, because of decreased competition and aggression between related or familiar neighbors (Greenwood et al. 1979, Waldman 1988, Eason and Hannon 1994).

Asymmetrical gene flow between islands groups may explain, in part, differences between island groups in the degree of genetic structuring. Gene flow estimates, calculated from mitochondrial DNA control region, 14 microsatellite loci, and two nuclear introns, indicate that more individuals are dispersing from Mikkelsen Bay to Simpson Lagoon (Sonsthagen et al. submitted a). Asymmetrical gene flow between island groups could generate a pattern of lower genetic structuring in the "source" population and clusters of more genetically related individuals in the "receiving" population coupled with unrelated individuals, as observed in our study. In the source population, females may be less able to nest in close proximity to kin because genetically-related individuals may have dispersed to the other island group. In the receiving population, females may nest in close proximity to kin, creating clusters of positive genetic autocorrelations; however, fewer clusters of positive autocorrelation may be observed because of random associations created with source population females.

Differences in genetic structure observed for Mikkelsen Bay between global distance class sampling and local autocorrelation analyses may be attributable to the spatial scale at which analyses were conducted. We may have not selected distance classes at an interval to detect structure among females. Distance intervals larger than actual spatial genetic structure would lead to failure to detect structure, whereas distance classes smaller than actual genetic structure would result in increased inter-individual variance and decrease the probability of detecting structure. Local autocorrelation analyses, however, are conducted among a focal female and her four nearest neighbors, irrespective of distance, and therefore, may be more biologically significant as analyses reflect genetic associations among females that are interacting with each other during nesting.

Conclusions

Common Eiders nesting on the coastal barrier islands in the Beaufort Sea nested in closer proximity to more genetically related individuals, creating clusters of non-random associations among individuals. Although we were able to detect significant microgeographic genetic structuring among nesting Common Eiders, this study likely underestimates the degree of relatedness, as not all females nesting on the study islands were sampled. Therefore, a female's nearest-neighbors for this study may not be the nearest individuals that a female interacted with during nest site selection. Finally, we cannot exclude the possibility that Common Eiders are nesting in close proximity to kin because of extreme natal philopatry rather than preferentially nesting close to kin. Long-term demographic data coupled with molecular techniques are needed to determine if the pattern of fine-scale genetic structuring observed in Beaufort Sea Common Eiders is because of extreme natal philopatry or female kin association.

Acknowledgments

Funding was provided by: Minerals Management Service (1435-01-98-CA-309); Coastal Marine Institute, University of Alaska Fairbanks; U.S. Geological Survey; Alaska EPSCoR Graduate Fellowship (NSF EPS-0092040); University of Alaska Foundation Angus Gavin Migratory Bird Research Fund; and BP Exploration (Alaska) Inc. We thank P. Flint, J. C. Franson, D. LaCroix, and J. Reed, U.S. Geological Survey, for providing samples, as well as; J. Gust and G. K. Sage, who provided laboratory assistance, and C. Monnett and J. Gleason, Minerals Management Service.

The USFWS banding number for the USGS is 20022 and the master permit holder is Dirk Derksen. The IACUC number #02-01 was assigned for this work to Kevin McCrackin.

Study Products

Manuscripts

Sonsthagen, S.A. 2006. Population genetic structure and phylogeography of Common Eiders (*Somateria mollissima*). Ph.D. dissertation. University of Alaska Fairbanks.

Sonsthagen, S.A., S.L. Talbot, R.B. Lanctot, K. Scribner, and K.G. McCracken. 2006. Population genetic structure of Common Eiders (*Somateria mollissima*) breeding in the Beaufort Sea, Alaska. Conservation Genetics. Submitted for peer-review.

Sonsthagen, S.A., S.L. Talbot, and K.G. McCracken. Genetic characterization of Common Eiders (*Somateria mollissima*) breeding in the Yukon-Kuskokwim Delta, Alaska. Condor. Submitted for peer-review.

Sonsthagen, S.A., J.R. Gust, G.K. Sage, S.L. Talbot, R. Tiedemann, and K.G. McCracken. 2006. Detection of sex-linkage in waterfowl "autosomal" microsatellite locus and its implication on an estimator of population differentiation. Molecular Ecology Notes. Submitted for peer-review.

Sonsthagen, S.A., S.L. Talbot, R.B. Lanctot, and K.G. McCracken. Do waterfowl nest in kin groups? Evidence from the Common Eider (*Somateria mollissima*) breeding in the Beaufort Sea, Alaska. Conservation Genetics. In prep.

Sonsthagen, S.A., S.L. Talbot, R.B. Lanctot, K. T. Scribner, and K.G. McCracken. Stepwise postglacial colonization of Common Eiders (*Somateria mollissima*) breeding in North America and Scandinavia. Molecular Ecology. In prep.

Sonsthagen, S.A., S.L. Talbot, R.B. Lanctot, K. T. Scribner, and K.G. McCracken. Multilocus population genetic structure of Common Eiders (*Somateria mollissima*) breeding in North America and Scandinavia. Molecular Ecology. In prep.

Sonsthagen, S.A., S.L. Talbot, R.B. Lanctot, K. T. Scribner, and K.G. McCracken. Diagnosibility of subspecies using a multilocus approach: An example from the Common Eider (*Somateria mollissima*). Molecular Ecology. In prep.

Sonsthagen, S.A., S.L. Talbot, R.B. Lanctot, and K.G. McCracken. Population genetic structure of Common Eiders (*Somateria mollissima*) breeding on the Aleutian Islands, Alaska. Condor. In prep.

Annual Reports

Sonsthagen, S.A., R.B. Lanctot, S.L. Talbot, K. Scribner, and K.G. McCracken. 2005. Population structure of Common Eiders nesting on the coastal barrier islands adjacent to oil facilities in the Beaufort Sea. Coastal Marine Institute Annual Report.

Sonsthagen, S.A., R.B. Lanctot, S.L. Talbot, K. Scribner, and K.G. McCracken. 2004. Population structure of Common Eiders nesting on the coastal barrier islands adjacent to oil facilities in the Beaufort Sea. Coastal Marine Institute Annual Report.

Sonsthagen, S.A., R.B. Lanctot, S.L. Talbot, K. Scribner, and K.G. McCracken. 2003. Population structure of Common Eiders nesting on the coastal barrier islands adjacent to oil facilities in the Beaufort Sea. Coastal Marine Institute Annual Report.

Sonsthagen, S.A., R.B. Lanctot, S.L. Talbot, K. Scribner, and K.G. McCracken. 2002. Population structure of Common Eiders nesting on the coastal barrier islands adjacent to oil facilities in the Beaufort Sea. Coastal Marine Institute Annual Report.

Oral Presentations

Sonsthagen, S.A., S.L. Talbot, R.B. Lanctot, K. Scribner, and K.G. McCracken. 2005. Population structure and phylogeography of Common Eiders. 2nd Annual North American Sea Duck Conference, Annapolis, Maryland.

Sonsthagen, S.A., S.L. Talbot, R.B. Lanctot, K. Scribner, and K.G. McCracken. 2005. Population structure of Common Eiders. Evolution Conference, Fairbanks, Alaska.

Sonsthagen, S.A., R.B. Lanctot, S.L. Talbot, K. Scribner, and K.G. McCracken. 2004. Population structure of Common Eiders breeding in North America and Scandinavia. Alaska Bird Conference, Anchorage, Alaska.

Poster Presentations

Sonsthagen, S.A., R.B. Lanctot, S.L. Talbot, K. Scribner, and K.G. McCracken. 2004. Population structure of Common Eiders breeding in North America and Scandinavia. 55th Arctic Science Conference, American Association for the Advancement of Science, Anchorage, Alaska.

Sonsthagen, S.A., R.B. Lanctot, S.L. Talbot, K. Scribner, and K.G. McCracken. 2003. Population structure of Common Eiders breeding in Alaska and Canada. North American Duck Symposium, Sacramento, California.

Sonsthagen, S.A., R.B. Lanctot, S.L. Talbot, K. Scribner, and K.G. McCracken. 2002. Population structure of Common Eiders nesting on the coastal barrier islands adjacent to oil facilities in the Beaufort Sea. North American Seaduck Conference and Workshop, Victoria, Canada.

Guest Presentations

Sonsthagen, S.A., R.B. Lanctot, S.L. Talbot, K. Scribner, and K.G. McCracken. 2006. Population structure of Common Eiders nesting on the coastal barrier islands adjacent to oil facilities in the Beaufort Sea. Coastal Marine Institute Annual Meeting, Fairbanks, Alaska.

Sonsthagen, S.A., R.B. Lanctot, S.L. Talbot, K. Scribner, and K.G. McCracken. 2005. Population structure of Common Eiders nesting on the coastal barrier islands adjacent to oil facilities in the Beaufort Sea. Mineral Management Service 10th Information Transfer Meeting, Anchorage, Alaska.

Sonsthagen, S.A., R.B. Lanctot, S.L. Talbot, K. Scribner, and K.G. McCracken. 2005. Population structure of Common Eiders nesting on the coastal barrier islands adjacent to oil facilities in the Beaufort Sea. Coastal Marine Institute Annual Meeting, Fairbanks, Alaska.

Sonsthagen, S.A., R.B. Lanctot, S.L. Talbot, K. Scribner, and K.G. McCracken. 2004. Population structure of Common Eiders nesting on the coastal barrier islands adjacent to oil facilities in the Beaufort

Sea. Coastal Marine Institute Annual Meeting, Fairbanks, Alaska.

Sonsthagen, S.A., R.B. Lanctot, S.L. Talbot, K. Scribner, and K.G. McCracken. 2003. Population structure of Common Eiders nesting on the coastal barrier islands adjacent to oil facilities in the Beaufort Sea. Coastal Marine Institute Annual Meeting, Fairbanks, Alaska.

References

Aasen E., J.F. Medrano and L. Sharrow. 1990. DNA extraction from nucleated red blood cells. Biotechniques 8(1):43.

Anderson, M.G., J.M. Rhymer and F.C. Rohwer. 1992. Philopatry, dispersal, and the genetic structure of waterfowl populations, p. 365–395. In B.D.J. Batt, A.D. Afton, M.G. Anderson, C.D. Ankney, D.H. Johnson, J.A. Kadlec and G.L. Krapu [eds.], Ecology and Management of Breeding Waterfowl. University of Minnesota Press, Minneapolis, Minnesota.

Avise, J.C. 2004. Molecular Markers, Natural History, and Evolution. Second Edition. Sinauer Associates, Inc., Sunderland, Massachusetts.

Belkhir, K., V. Castric and F. Bonhomme. 2002. IDENTIX, a software to test for relatedness in a population using permutation methods. Mol. Ecol. Notes 2(4):611–614. doi:10.1046/j.1471-8286.2002.00273.x

Bonnet, E., and Y. Van de Peer. 2002. zt: A software tool for simple and partial Mantel tests. J. Stat. Softw. 7(10):1–12.

Buchholz, W.G., J.M. Pearce, B.J. Pierson and K.T. Scribner. 1998. Dinucleotide repeat polymorphisms in waterfowl (family Anatidae): Characterization of a sex-linked (Z-specific) and 14 autosomal loci. Anim. Genet. 29(4):323–325.

Bustness, J.O., and K.E. Erikstad. 1993. Site fidelity in breeding Common Eider Somateria mollissima females. Ornis Fennica 70:11–16.

Double, M.C., R. Peakall, N.R. Beck and A. Cockburn. 2005. Dispersal, philopatry, and infidelity: Dissecting local genetic structure in superb fairy-wrens (Malurus cyaneus). Evolution 59(3):625–635.

Cooch, F.G. 1965. The breeding biology and management of the northern eider (Somateria mollissima borealis), Cape Dorset, NWT. Can. Wildl. Serv. Wildl. Manage. Bull. Ser. 2., No. 10, Ottawa, Ontario.

Eason. P., and S.J. Hannon. 1994. New birds on the block: New neighbors increase defensive costs for territorial male willow ptarmigan. Behav. Ecol. Sociobiol. 34(6):419–426. doi: 10.1007/BF00167333

Fowler, A.C., J.M. Eadie and C.R. Ely. 2004. Relatedness and nesting dispersion within breeding populations of Greater White-Fronted Geese. Condor 106(3):600–607. doi: 10.1650/7446

Goudet, J. 1995. FSTAT (version 1.2): A computer program to calculate F-statistics. J. Heredity 86(6):485–486.

Goudet, J. 2001. FSTAT, a program to estimate and test gene diversities and fixation indices (version 2.9.3.2). Available at http://www2.unil.ch/popgen/softwares/fstat htm (accessed 7 July 2004).

Goudie, R.I., G.J. Robertson and A. Reed. 2000. Common Eider (Somateria mollissima), The Birds of North America, No. 546 [A. Poole and F. Gill, eds.]. The Birds of North America, Inc., Philadelphia, Pennsylvania, 32 p.

Greenwood, P.J., P.H. Harvey and C.M. Perrins. 1979. The role of dispersal in the great tit (Parus major): The causes, consequences and heritability of natal dispersal. J. Anim. Ecol. 48(1):123–142.

Hatchwell, B.J., D.J. Ross, M.K. Fowlie and A. McGowan. 2001. Kin discrimination in cooperatively breeding long-tailed tits. Proc. R. Soc. B 268(1470):885–890. doi: 10.1098/rspb.2001.1598

Johnson, S.R. 2000. Pacific Eider, p. 259–275. In J.C. Truett and S.R. Johnson [eds.], The Natural History of an Arctic Oil Field: Development and the Biota. Academic Press, San Diego, California.

Koenig, W.D., D. Van Vuran and P.N. Hooge. 1996. Detectability, philopatry, and the distribution of dispersal distances in vertebrates. Trends Ecol. Evol. 11(12):514–517. doi:10.1016/S0169-5347(96)20074-6

Komdeur, J., and B.J. Hatchwell. 1999. Kin recognition: Function and mechanism in avian species. Trends Ecol. Evol. 14(6):237–241. doi:10.1016/S0169-5347(98)01573-0

Komdeur, J., D.S. Richardson and T. Burke. 2004. Experimental evidence that kin discrimination in the Seychelles warbler is based on association and not on genetic relatedness. Proc. R. Soc. B 271(1542):963–969. doi: 10.1098/rspb.2003.2665

Lessells, C.M., M.I. Avery and J.R. Krebs. 1994. Nonrandom dispersal of kin: Why do European bee-eater (Merops apiaster) brothers nest close together? Behav. Ecol. 5(1):105–113. doi:10.1093/beheco/5.1.105

Longmire, J.L., A.K. Lewis, N.C. Brown, J.M. Buckingham, L.M. Clark, M.D. Jones, L.J. Meincke, J. Meyne, R.L. Ratliff, F.A. Ray, R.P. Wagner and R.K. Moyzis. 1988. Isolation and molecular characterization of a highly polymorphic centromeric tandem repeat in the family Falconidae. Genomics 2(1):14–24.

Maak, S., K. Neumann, G. von Lengerken and R. Gattermann. 2000. First seven microsatellites developed for the Peking duck (Anas platyrhynchos). Anim. Genet. 31(3):233.

Maak, S., K. Wimmers, S. Weigend and K. Neumann. 2003. Isolation and characterization of 18 microsatellites in the Peking duck (Anas platyrhynchos) and their application in other waterfowl species. Mol. Ecol. Notes 3(2):224–227. doi: 10.1046/j.1471-8286.2003.00405.x

McKinnon, L. 2005. Female sociality in the common eider (Somateria mollissima). M.S. Thesis, Michigan State Univ., East Lansing, Michigan, 51 p.

Noel, L.E., S.R. Johnson, G.M. O'Doherty and M.K. Butcher. 2005. Common Eider (Somateria mollissima v-nigrum) nest cover and depredation on central Alaskan Beaufort Sea barrier islands. Arctic 58(2):129–136.

Öst, M., E. Vitikainen, P. Waldeck, L. Sundström, K. Lindström, T. Hollmén, J.C. Franson and M. Kilpi. 2005. Eider females from non-kin brood-rearing coalitions. Mol. Ecol. 14(12):3903–3908. doi:10.1111/j.1365-294X.2005.02694.x

Paulus, K.B., and R. Tiedemann. 2003. Ten polymorphic autosomal microsatellite loci for the Eider duck Somateria mollissima and their cross-species applicability among waterfowl species (Anatidae). Mol. Ecol. Notes 3(2):250–252. doi: 10.1046/j.1471-8286.2003.00414.x

Peakall, R., and P.E. Smouse. 2006. GENALEX 6: Genetic analysis in Excel. Population genetic software for teaching and research. Mol. Ecol. Notes 6(1):288–295. doi:10.1111/j.1471-8286.2005.01155.x

Pearce, J.M., S.L. Talbot, M.R. Petersen and J.R. Rearick. 2005. Limited genetic differentiation among breeding, molting, and wintering groups of threatened Steller's eider: The role of historic and contemporary factors. Conserv. Genet. 6(5):743–757.

Queller, D.C., and K.F. Goodnight. 1989. Estimating relatedness using genetic markers. Evolution 43(2):258–275.

Raymond, M., and F. Rousset. 1995. GENEPOP (version 1.2): Population genetics software for exact tests and ecumenicism. J. Heredity 86(3):248–249.

Sayler, J.W. 1962. A bow-net trap for ducks. J. Wildl. Manage. 26(2):219–221.

Schmutz, J.F., R.J. Robertson and F. Cooke. 1983. Colonial nesting of the Hudson Bay eider duck. Can. J. Zool. 61(11):2424–2433.

Scribner, K.T., M.R. Petersen, R.L. Fields, S.L. Talbot, J.M. Pearce and R.K. Chesser. 2001. Sex-biased gene flow in Spectacled Eiders (Anatidae): Inferences from molecular markers with contracting modes of inheritance. Evolution 55(10):2105–2115.

Smouse, P.E., and R. Peakall. 1999. Spatial autocorrelation analysis of individual multiallele and multilocus genetic structure. Heredity 82(5):561–573.

Sonsthagen, S.A., S.L. Talbot, R.B. Lanctot, K.T. Scribner and K.G. McCracken. Submitted a. Population genetic structure of Common Eiders (Somateria mollissima) breeding in the Beaufort Sea, Alaska. Conserv. Genet.

Sonsthagen, S.A., S.L. Talbot, R.B. Lanctot, K.T. Scribner and K.G. McCracken. Submitted b. Multilocus phylogeography and population structure of Common Eiders breeding in North America and Scandinavia. Mol. Ecol.

Sonsthagen, S.A., S.L. Talbot and C.M. White. 2004. Gene flow and genetic characterization of Northern Goshawks breeding in Utah. Condor 106(4):826–836. doi: 10.1650/7448

Swennen, C. 1990. Dispersal and migratory movements of eiders Somateria mollissima breeding in the Netherlands. Ornis Scand. 21(1):17–27.

Tiedemann, R., K.B. Paulus, M. Scheer, K.G. von Kistowski, K. Skírnisson, D. Bloch and M. Dam. 2004. Mitochondrial DNA and microsatellite variation in the eider duck (Somateria mollissima) indicate stepwise postglacial colonization of Europe and limited current long-distance dispersal. Mol. Ecol. 13(6):1481–1494. doi:10.1111/j.1365-294X.2004.02168.x

Tiedemann, R., K.G. von Kistowski and H. Noer. 1999. On sex-specific dispersal and mating tactics in the Common Eider Somateria mollissima as inferred from the genetic structure of breeding colonies. Behaviour 136(9):1145–1155.

Valière, N. 2002. GIMLET: A computer program for analysing genetic individual identification data. Mol. Ecol. Notes 2(3):377–379.

van der Jeugd, H.P., I.T. van der Veen and K. Larsson. 2002. Kin clustering in barnacle geese: Familiarity or phenotype matching? Behav. Ecol. 13(6):786–790. doi:10.1093/beheco/13.6.786

Waldman, B. 1988. The ecology of kin recognition. Ann. Rev. Ecol. Syst. 19:543–571.

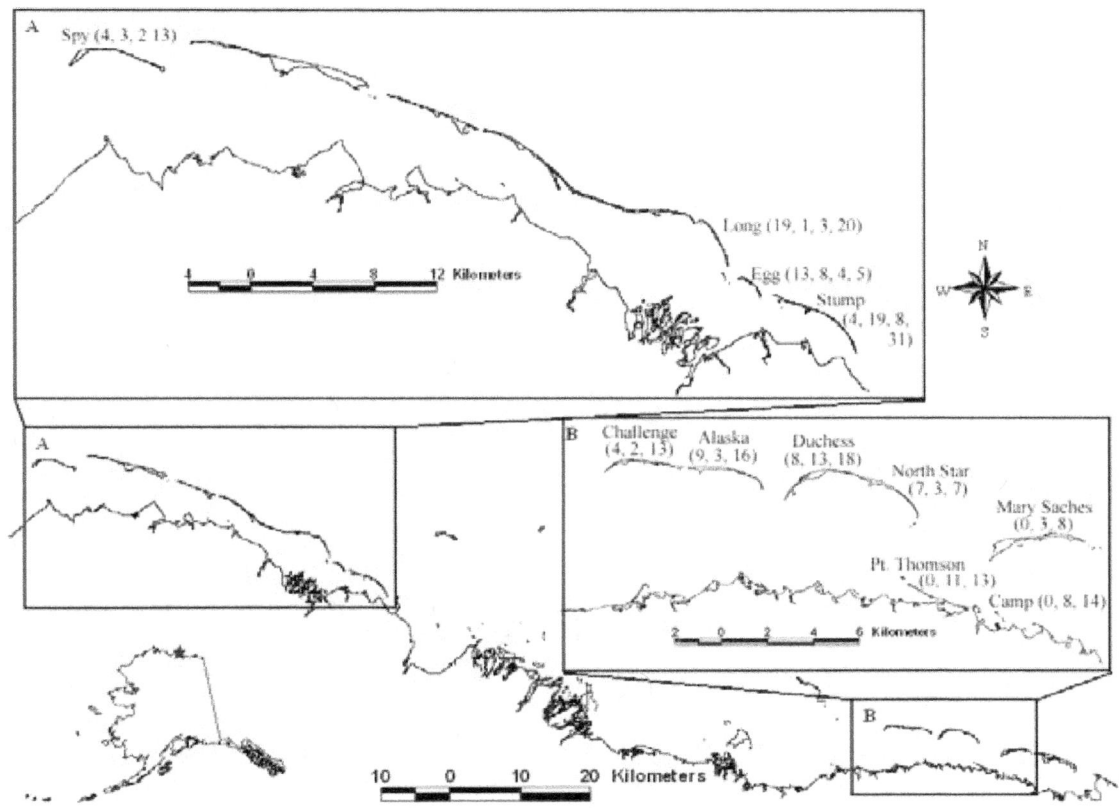

Figure 3.1: Beaufort Sea barrier islands located in (A) Simpson Lagoon (western group) and (B) Mikkelsen Bay (eastern group) with samples sizes for each island in a given year in parentheses; 2000–2003, respectively; no samples were collected in 2001 for Mikkelsen Bay. Camp designation is used by the authors and is not the official name of the island.

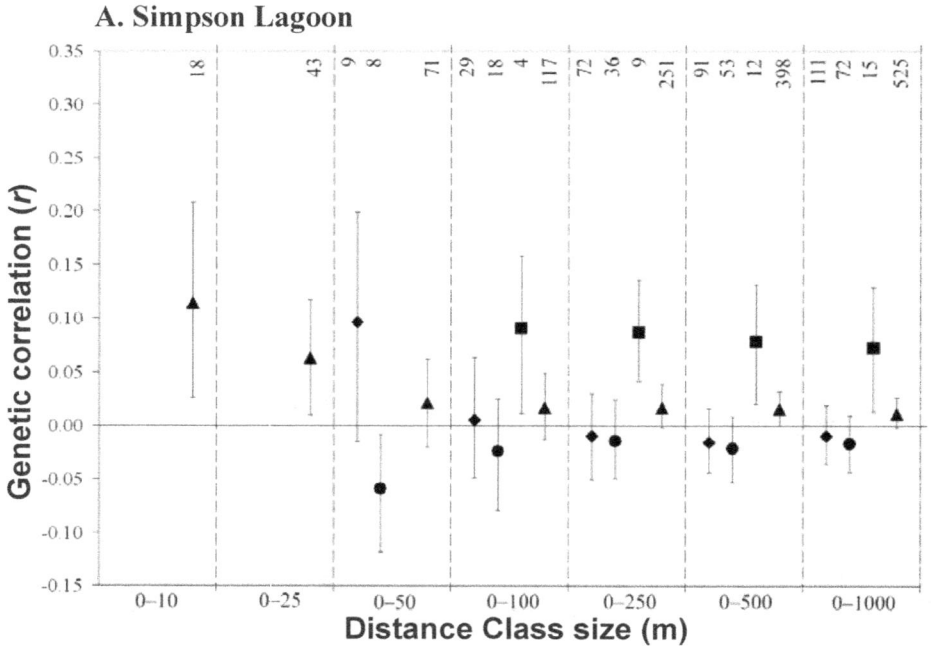

A. Simpson Lagoon

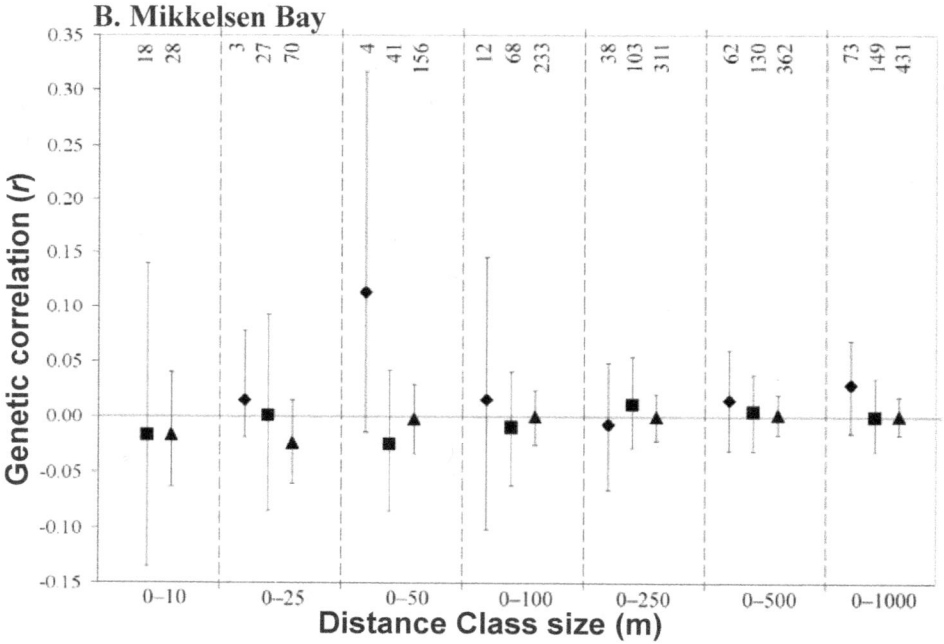

B. Mikkelsen Bay

Figure 3.2: Genetic correlation (*r*) of females breeding in (A) Simpson Lagoon and (B) Mikkelsen Bay at increasing distance class size intervals. Symbols represent females breeding in 2000 (diamonds), 2001 (circles), 2002 (squares), and 2003 (triangles). Number of pairwise comparisons for each distance class is shown above the plotted values. The 95% confidence error bars about *r* were estimated by bootstrapping.

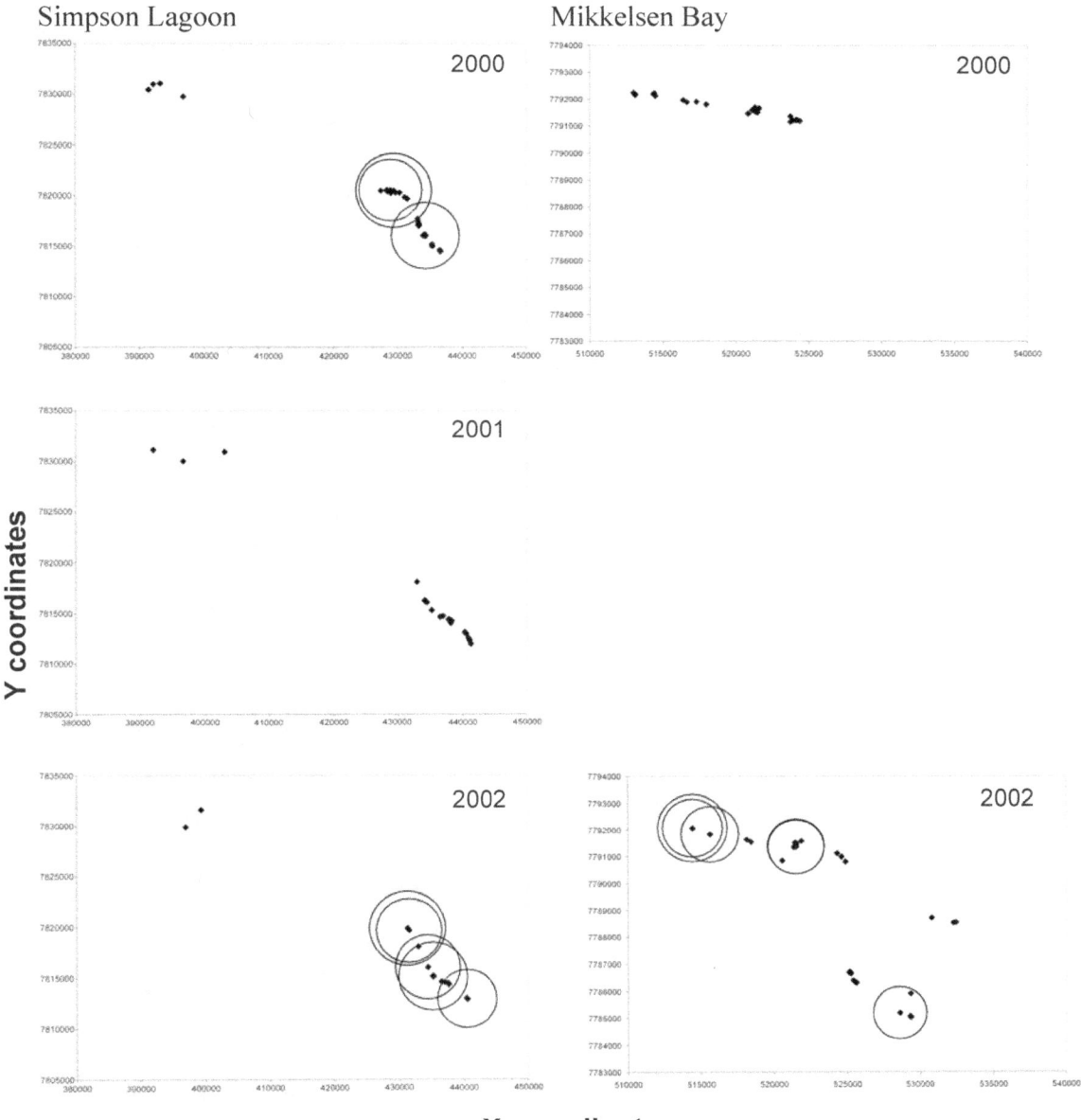

Figure 3.3: Bubble plots of two-dimensional local spatial autocorrelation analysis of Common Eider females nesting in Simpson Lagoon and Mikkelsen Bay in 2000–2003. Each plot shows the study area with squares indicating the nest location. Bubbles surround the nests with positive *Ir* values, based on the four nearest neighbors, and within 5% tail of the permutated distribution. The size of the circle is proportional to the magnitude of *Ir*.

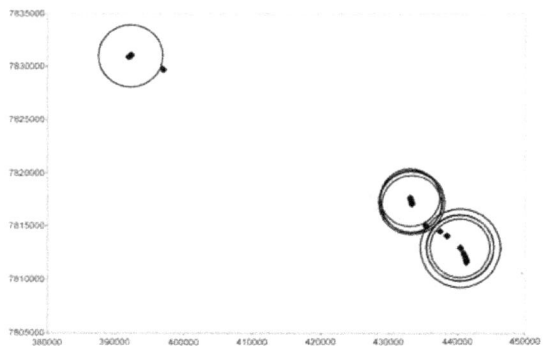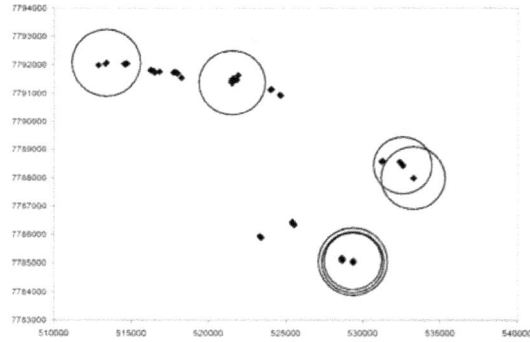

Figure 3.3 cont.

Table 3.1: Number of alleles, fragment length, observed heterozygosity (H_o), and probability of identity among randomly mating individuals (PID), and siblings (PID_{sib}) for 14 microsatellite loci.

Locus	Number of alleles	Fragment length	H_o	PID	PID_{sib}
*Aph*02	4	110–116	0.516	1/3.52	1/1.82
*Aph*08	3	138–142	0.459	1/2.53	1/1.61
*Aph*20	9	162–184	0.645	1/5.90	1/2.20
*Aph*23	7	206–218	0.599	1/5.10	1/2.60
*Cm*09	9	102–124	0.599	1/4.89	1/1.99
*Bca*µ1	4	108–114	0.451	1/2.97	1/1.59
*Bca*µ11	7	135–147	0.395	1/2.54	1/1.54
*Hhi*µ3	3	110–114	0.119	1/1.61	1/1.26
*Sfi*µ10	19	129–181	0.875	1/38.87	1/3.13
*Smo*4	44	155–257	0.918	1/251.38	1/3.63
*Smo*7	6	197–213	0.362	1/2.57	1/1.55
*Smo*8	7	115–127	0.625	1/4.90	1/2.00
*Smo*10	21	115–163	0.782	1/14.87	1/2.62
*Smo*12	15	100–117	0.729	1/11.84	1/2.50
Total loci	–	–	0.577	3.21×10^{-12}	5.34×10^{-5}

Table 3.2: Average number of alleles, observed and expected heterozygosities (H_o/H_e), overall relatedness values (r_{xy}; Queller and Goodnight 1989) with variances, and sample sizes (n) for Common Eiders breeding on two island groups (Simpson Lagoon and Mikkelsen Bay) in the Beaufort Sea, Alaska, in 2000–2003.

	No. alleles	H_o/H_e (%)	r_{xy}	variance	n
Simpson Lagoon					
2000	7.36	59.5/59.5	−0.026	0.033	40
2001	7.29	60.1/60.3	−0.033	0.029	31
2002	6.21	60.6/58.3	−0.063	0.039	17
2003	8.64	56.1/59.3	−0.014	0.037	69
Mikkelsen Bay					
2000	6.64	58.2/58.5	−0.037	0.036	28
2002	8.00	57.3/59.8	−0.021	0.042	43
2003	8.79	56.1/58.6	−0.008	0.037	89

Table 3.3: Pearson correlation values (*r*) for genetic distance (GD) and relatedness values (r_{xy}) and geographic distance for female Common Eiders nesting on two island groups (Simpson Lagoon and Mikkelsen Bay) in the Beaufort Sea, Alaska, in 2000–2003. Significant correlations ($P < 0.001$) are in bold text.

	2000	2001	2002	2003
Simpson Lagoon				
r–GD	**0.534**	**0.608**	**0.579**	**0.616**
r–r_{xy}	**−0.088**	**−0.047**	**−0.168**	**−0.033**
Mikkelsen Bay				
r–GD	**0.786**	–	**0.800**	**0.813**
r–r_{xy}	**−0.181**	–	**−0.032**	**−0.012**

Table 3.4. Local autocorrelation (*lr*) values and percent of nesting females from Simpson Lagoon and Mikkelsen Bay in 2000–2003 with positive genetic correlation among a focal individual and her four nearest neighbors.

	2000	2001	2002	2003
Simpson Lagoon				
Positive *lr*	0.141–0.176	–	0.098–0.159	0.137–0.250
	8% (*n* = 3/40)		29% (*n* = 5/17)	13% (*n* = 9/69)
Mikkelsen Bay				
Positive *lr*	–	–	0.139–0.232	0.124–0.180
			14% (*n* = 6/43)	8% (*n* = 7/89)